Conversations with God

an uncommon dialogue

Conversations with God

• an uncommon dialogue •

book 1

Neale Donald Walsch

G. P. PUTNAM'S SONS

NEW YORK

G. P. Putnam's Sons
Publishers Since 1838
200 Madison Avenue
New York, New York 10016

FIRST HARDCOVER EDITION 1996
Originally published by Hampton Roads Publishing
Company, Inc., 1995

Library of Congress Cataloging-in-Publication Data

Walsch, Neale Donald.
Conversations with God: an uncommon dialogue/Neale Donald
Walsch.
p.   cm.
ISBN 0-399-14278-9 (alk. paper)
1. God—Miscellanea.   2. Spiritual life—Miscellanea.
3. Imaginary conversations.   4. Walsch, Neale Donald.
I. Title.
BF1999.W228   1996   96-34667   CIP
133.9'3—dc20

Printed in the United States of America
1   3   5   7   9   10   8   6   4   2
This book is printed on acid-free paper. ∞

Acknowledgments

First, last, and always, I want to acknowledge the Source of everything that is in this book, everything that is life—and of life itself.

Second, I want to thank my spiritual teachers, who include the saints and sages of all religions.

Third, it is clear to me that all of us could produce a list of people who have touched our lives in ways so meaningful and so profoundly as to defy categorization or description; people who have shared with us their wisdom, told us their truth, suffered us our faults and our foibles in their infinite patience, and who have seen us through all of it; seeing the best in us there was to see. People who, in their acceptance of us, as well as their *refusal* to accept the parts of us they knew we really didn't choose, caused us to grow; to get *bigger* somehow.

The people, in addition to my parents, who have been there for me in that way include Samantha Gorski, Tara-Jenelle Walsch, Wayne Davis, Bryan Walsch, Martha Wright, the late Ben Wills, Jr., Roland Chambers, Dan Higgs, C. Berry Carter II, Ellen Moyer, Anne Blackwell, Dawn Dancing Free, Ed Keller, Lyman W. (Bill) Griswold, Elisabeth Kübler-Ross, and dear, dear Terry Cole-Whittaker.

I want to include in this group my former mates, whose privacy I wish to respect by not naming them here, but whose contributions to my life are deeply grasped and appreciated.

And as gratitude for the gifts I have received from all these wonderful people swells my heart, I am especially warmed by the thought of my helpmate, spouse, and partner, Nancy Fleming Walsch, a woman of extraordinary wisdom, compassion and love, who has shown me that my highest thoughts about human relationships do not have to remain fantasies, but can be dreams come true.

Fourth and finally, I want to recognize some people I have never met, but whose lives and work have impacted me with such force that I cannot let this moment pass without thanking them from the depth of my being for the moments of exquisite pleasure, insight into the human condition, and pure, simple *Lifegefeelkin* (I made up that word!) they have given me.

You know what it is like when someone has given you a taste, a glorious moment, of what *is really true about life?* For me, most of these have been creative or performing artists, because it is from art that I receive inspiration, to which I retreat in moments of reflection, and in which I find that which we call God most beautifully expressed.

And so I want to thank. . .John Denver, whose songs touch my soul and fill it with new hope about how life could be; Richard Bach, whose writings reach into my life as if they were my own, describing so much of what has been my experience; Barbra Streisand, whose directing, acting, and musical artistry grips my heart time and time again, causing it to *feel* what is true, not merely know it; and the late Robert Heinlein, whose visionary literature has raised questions and posed answers in ways no one else has dared even approach.

For

ANNE M. WALSCH

Who not only taught me that God exists,
but opened my mind to the wondrous truth
that God is my best friend;
and who was far more than a mother to me,
but gave birth *in* me
to a longing for and a love of God,
and all that is good.
Mom was
my first meeting
with an angel.

And for

ALEX M. WALSCH

Who told me repeatedly throughout my life,
"There's nothing to it,"
"You don't have to take No for an answer,"
"You make your own luck,"
and
"There's more where that came from."
Dad was
my first experience
of fearlessness.

Introduction

You are about to have an extraordinary experience. You are about to have a conversation with God. Yes, yes. I know. . .that's not possible. You probably think (or have been taught) *that's not possible*. One can talk *to* God, sure, but not *with* God. I mean, God is not going to *talk back*, right? At least not in the form of a regular, everyday kind of conversation!

That's what I thought, too. Then this book happened to me. And I mean that literally. This book was not written *by* me, it happened *to* me. And in your reading of it, it will happen to you, for *we are all led to the truth for which we are ready.*

My life would probably be much easier if I had kept all of this quiet. Yet that wasn't the reason it happened to me. And whatever inconveniences the book may cause me (such as being called a blasphemer, a fraud, a hypocrite for not having lived these truths in the past, or—perhaps worse—a holy man), it is not possible for me to stop the process now. Nor do I wish to. I have had my chances to step away from this whole thing, and I haven't taken them. I've decided to stick with what my instincts are telling me, rather than what much of the world will tell me, about the material here.

Those instincts say this book is not nonsense, the overworking of a frustrated spiritual imagination, or simply the self-justification of a man seeking vindication from a life misled. Oh, I've thought of all of those things—every one of them. So I gave this material to a few people to read while it was still in manuscript form. They were moved. And they cried. And they laughed for the joy and the humor in it. And their lives, they said, changed. They were transfixed. They were empowered.

Many said they were transformed.

That's when I knew this book was for everyone, and that it *had* to be published; for it is a wonderful gift to all those who truly want answers and who truly care about the questions; for all those who have embarked upon quests for truth with sincerity of heart, longing of soul, and openness of mind. And that's pretty much _all of us_.

This book addresses most, if not all, of the questions we have ever asked about life and love, purpose and function, people and relationships, good and evil, guilt and sin, forgiveness and redemption, the path to God and the road to hell. . .everything. It directly discusses sex, power, money, children, marriage, divorce, life work, health, the hereafter, the before-now. . ._everything_. It explores war and peace, knowing and not knowing, giving and taking, joy and sorrow. It looks at the concrete and the abstract, the visible and the invisible, the truth and the untruth.

You could say that this book is "God's latest word on things," although some people might have a little trouble with that, particularly if they think that God stopped talking 2,000 years ago or that, if God _has_ continued communicating, it's been only with holy men, medicine women, or someone who has been meditating for 30 years, or good for 20, or at least half-decent for 10 (none of which categories includes me).

The truth is, God talks to everybody. The good and the bad. The saint and the scoundrel. And certainly all of us in between. Take you, for instance. God has come to you many ways in your life, and this is another of them. How many times have you heard the old axiom: When the student is ready, the teacher will appear? This book is our teacher.

Shortly after this material began happening to me, I knew that I was talking with God. Directly, personally. Irrefutably. And that God was responding to my questions in direct proportion to my ability to comprehend. That is, I was being answered in ways, and with language, that God knew I would understand. This accounts for much of the colloquial style of the writing and the occasional references to material I'd gathered from other sources and prior experiences in my life. I know now that everything that has ever come to me in my life _has come to me from God_, and it was now being drawn together, pulled together, in a magnificent, complete response to _every question I ever had_.

And somewhere along the way I realized a book was being produced—a book intended for publication. Indeed, I was told specifically during the latter part of the dialogue (in February 1993) that *three* books would actually be produced, and that:

1. The first would deal mainly with personal topics, focusing on an individual's life challenges and opportunities.
2. The second would deal with more global topics of geo-political and metaphysical life on the planet, and the challenges now facing the world.
3. The third would deal with universal truths of the highest order, and the challenges and opportunities of the soul.

This is the first of those books, completed in February 1993. For clarity I should explain that, as I transcribed this dialogue by hand, I underlined or circled words and sentences which came to me with particular emphasis—as if God were booming them out—and these were later placed in italics by the typesetter.

I need now to say that I am—having read and reread the wisdom contained here—deeply embarrassed by my own life, which has been marked by continued mistakes and misdeeds, some very shameful behaviors, and some choices and decisions which I'm certain others consider hurtful and unforgivable. Though I have profound remorse that it was through others' pain, I am unspeakably grateful for all that I have learned, and found that I have still *yet* to learn, because of the people in my life. I apologize to everybody for the slowness of that learning. Yet I am encouraged by God to grant myself forgiveness for my failings and not to live in fear and guilt but to always keep trying—keep on trying—to live a grander vision.

I know that's what God wants for all of us.

Neale Donald Walsch
Central Point, Oregon
Christmas 1994

Conversations with God
an uncommon dialogue

1

In the spring of 1992—it was around Easter as I recall—an extraordinary phenomenon occurred in my life. God began talking with you. Through me.

Let me explain.

I was very unhappy during that period, personally, professionally, and emotionally, and my life was feeling like a failure on all levels. As I'd been in the habit for years of writing my thoughts down in letters (which I usually never delivered), I picked up my trusty yellow legal pad and began pouring out my feelings.

This time, rather than another letter to another person I imagined to be victimizing me, I thought I'd go straight to the source; straight to the greatest victimizer of them all. I decided to write a letter to God.

It was a spiteful, passionate letter, full of confusions, contortions, and condemnations. And a *pile* of angry questions.

Why wasn't my life working? What would it take to *get* it to work? Why could I not find happiness in relationships? Was the experience of adequate money going to elude me forever? Finally—and most emphatically—*What had I done to deserve a life of such continuing struggle?*

To my surprise, as I scribbled out the last of my bitter, unanswerable questions and prepared to toss my pen aside, my hand remained poised over the paper, as if held there by some invisible force. Abruptly, the pen began *moving on its own.* I had no idea what I was about to write, but an idea seemed to be coming, so I decided to flow with it. Out came. . .

Do you really want an answer to all these questions, or are you just venting?

I blinked. . .and then my mind came up with a reply. I wrote that down, too.

Both. I'm venting, sure, but if these questions have answers, I'd sure as hell like to hear them!

You are "sure as hell". . .about a lot of things. But wouldn't it be nice to be "sure as *Heaven*"?

And I wrote:
What is that supposed to mean?

Before I knew it, I had begun a conversation. . .and I was not writing so much as *taking dictation*.

That dictation went on for three years, and at the time, I had no idea where it was going. The answers to the questions I was putting on paper never came to me until the question was completely written and I'd put my *own thoughts away*. Often the answers came faster than I could write, and I found myself scribbling to keep up. When I became confused, or lost the feeling that the words were coming from somewhere else, I put the pen down and walked away from the dialogue until I again felt inspired—sorry, that's the only word which truly fits—to return to the yellow legal pad and start transcribing again.

These conversations are still going on as I write this. And much of it is found on the pages which follow. . .pages which contain an astounding dialogue which at first I disbelieved, then assumed to be of personal value, but which I now understand was meant for more than just me. It was meant for you and everyone else who has come to this material. For my questions are your questions.

I want you to get into this dialogue as soon as you can, because what's really important here is not *my* story, but *yours*. It is *your* life story which brought you here. It is *your* personal experience to which this material has relevance. Otherwise you would not be here, with it, right now.

So let's enter the dialogue with a question I had been asking for a very long time: How does God talk, and to whom? When I asked this question, here's the answer I received:

I talk to everyone. All the time. The question is not to whom do I talk, but who listens?

Intrigued, I asked God to expand on this subject. Here's what God said:

First, let's exchange the word *talk* with the word *communicate*. It's a much better word, a much fuller, more accurate one. When we try to speak to each other—Me to you, you to Me, we are immediately constricted by the unbelievable limitation of words. For this reason, I do not communicate by words alone. In fact, rarely do I do so. My most common form of communication is through *feeling*.

Feeling is the language of the soul.

If you want to know what's true for you about something, look to how you're *feeling* about it.

Feelings are sometimes difficult to discover—and often even more difficult to acknowledge. Yet hidden in your deepest feelings is your highest truth.

The trick is to get to those feelings. I will show you how. Again. If you wish.

I told God that I did wish, but that right now I wished even more for a complete and full answer to my first question. Here's what God said:

I also communicate with *thought*. Thought and feelings are not the same, although they can occur at the same time. In communicating with thought, I often use images and pictures. For this reason, thoughts are more effective than mere words as tools of communication.

In addition to feelings and thoughts, I also use the vehicle of *experience* as a grand communicator.

And finally, when feelings and thoughts and experience all fail, I use *words*. Words are really the least effective communicator. They are most open to misinterpretation, most often misunderstood.

And why is that? It is because of what words *are*. Words are merely utterances: *noises* that *stand for* feelings, thoughts, and experience. They are symbols. Signs. Insignias. They are not Truth. They are not the real thing.

Words may help you understand something. Experience allows you to know. Yet there are some things you cannot experience. So I have given you other tools of knowing. And these are called feelings. And so too, thoughts.

Now the supreme irony here is that you have all placed so much importance on the Word of God, and so little on the experience.

In fact, you place so little value on experience that when what you *experience* of God differs from what you've *heard* of God, you automatically *discard the experience and own the words,* when it should be just the other way around.

Your experience and your feelings about a thing represent what you factually and intuitively know about that thing. Words can only seek to *symbolize* what you know, and can often *confuse* what you know.

These, then, are the tools with which I communicate, yet they are not the methods, for not all feelings, not all thoughts, not all experience, and not all words are from Me.

Many words have been uttered by others, in My name. Many thoughts and many feelings have been sponsored by causes not of My direct creation. Many experiences result from these.

The challenge is one of discernment. The difficulty is knowing the difference between messages from God and data from other sources. Discrimination is a simple matter with the application of a basic rule:

Mine is always your Highest Thought, your Clearest Word, your Grandest Feeling. Anything less is from another source.

Now the task of differentiation becomes easy, for it should not be difficult even for the beginning student to identify the Highest, the Clearest, and the Grandest.

Yet will I give you these guidelines:

The Highest Thought is always that thought which contains joy. The Clearest Words are those words which contain truth. The Grandest Feeling is that feeling which you call love.

Joy, truth, love.

These three are interchangeable, and one always leads to the other. It matters not in which order they are placed.

Having with these guidelines determined which messages are Mine and which have come from another source, the only question remaining is whether My messages will be heeded.

Most of My messages are not. Some, because they seem too good to be true. Others, because they seem too difficult to follow. Many, because they are simply misunderstood. Most, because they are not received.

My most powerful messenger is experience, and even this you ignore. *Especially* this you ignore.

Your world would not be in its present condition were you to have simply listened to your experience. The result of your *not* listening to your experience is that you keep re-living it, over and over again. For My purpose will not be thwarted, nor My will be ignored. You *will* get the message. Sooner or later.

I will not force you to, however. I will never coerce you. For I have given you a free will—the power to do as you choose—and I will never take that away from you, ever.

And so I will continue sending you the same messages over and over again, throughout the millennia and to whatever corner of the universe you occupy. Endlessly will I send you My messages, until you have received them and held them close, calling them your own.

My messages will come in a hundred forms, at a thousand moments, across a million years. You cannot miss them if you truly listen. You cannot ignore them once truly heard. Thus will our communication begin in earnest. For in the past you have only talked _to_ Me, praying to Me, interceding with Me, beseeching Me. Yet now can I talk _back_ to you, even as I am doing here.

How can I know this communication is from God? How do I know this is not my own imagination?

What would be the difference? Do you not see that I could just as easily work through your imagination as anything else? I will bring you the exact right thoughts, words or feelings, at any given moment, suited precisely to the purpose at hand, using one device, or several.

You will know these words are from Me because you, of your own accord, have never spoken so clearly. Had you already spoken so clearly on these questions, you would not be asking them.

To whom does God communicate? Are there special people? Are there special times?

All people are special, and all moments are golden. There is no person and there is no time one more special than another. Many people choose to believe that God communicates in special ways and only with special people. This removes the mass of the people from responsibility for hearing My message, much less _receiving_ it (which is another matter), and allows them to take someone else's word for everything. You don't _have_ to listen to Me, for you've already decided that others have heard from Me on every subject, and you have _them_ to listen to.

By listening to what _other_ people think they heard Me say, _you_ don't have to _think at all._

This is the biggest reason for most people turning

from My messages on a personal level. If you acknowledge that you are receiving My messages *directly*, then
you are responsible for interpreting them. It is far safer
and much easier to accept the interpretation of others
(even others who have lived 2,000 years ago) than seek
to interpret the message you may very well be receiving
in this moment now.

Yet I invite you to a new form of communication
with God. A *two-way* communication. In truth, it is you
who have invited Me. For I have come to you, in this
form, right now, in *answer to your call.*

Why do some people, take Christ, for example, seem to hear
more of Your communication than others?

Because some people are willing to actually listen.
They are willing to hear, and they are willing to remain
open to the communication even when it seems scary,
or crazy, or downright wrong.

We should listen to God even when what's being said seems
wrong?

Especially when it seems wrong. If you think you are
right about everything, who needs to talk with God?

Go ahead and act on all that you know. But notice
that you've all been doing that since time began. And
look at what shape the world is in. Clearly, you've
missed something. Obviously, there is something you
don't understand. That which you *do* understand must
seem right to you, because "right" is a term you use to
designate something with which you agree. What
you've missed will, therefore, appear at first to be
"wrong."

The only way to move forward on this is to ask
yourself, "What would happen if everything I thought
was 'wrong' was actually 'right'?" Every great scientist
knows about this. When what a scientist does is not

working, a scientist sets aside all of the assumptions and starts over. All great discoveries have been made from a willingness, and ability, to *not be right*. And that's what's needed here.

You cannot know God until you've stopped telling yourself that you *already* know God. You cannot hear God until you stop thinking that you've already heard God.

I cannot tell you My Truth until you stop telling Me yours.

But my truth about God comes from *You.*

Who said so?

Others.

What others?

Leaders. Ministers. Rabbis. Priests. Books. The *Bible,* for heaven's sake!

Those are not authoritative sources.

They *aren't?*

No.

Then what *is?*

Listen to your *feelings.* Listen to your Highest Thoughts. Listen to your experience. Whenever any one of these differ from what you've been told by your teachers, or read in your books, forget the words. *Words are the least reliable purveyor of Truth.*

There is so much I want to say to You, so much I want to ask. I don't know where to begin.

For instance, why is it that You do not reveal Yourself? If there really is a God, and You are It, why do You not reveal Yourself in a way we can all understand?

I have done so, over and over. I am doing so again right now.

No. I mean by a method of revelation that is incontrovertible; that cannot be denied.

Such as?

Such as appearing right now before my eyes.

I am doing so right now.

Where?

Everywhere you look.

No, I mean in an incontrovertible way. In a way no man could deny.

What way would that be? In what form or shape would you have Me appear?

In the form or shape that you actually have.

That would be impossible, for I have no form or shape you understand. I could *adopt* a form or shape that you *could* understand, but then everyone would assume that what they have seen is the one and only form and shape of God, rather than *a* form or shape of God—one of many.

People believe I am what they see Me as, rather than what they do *not* see. But I am the Great Unseen, not what I cause Myself to be in any particular moment. In a sense, I am what I *am not*. It is from the *am-notness* that I come, and to it I always return.

Yet when I come in one particular form or another—a form in which I think people can understand Me—people *assign Me that form forevermore.*

And should I come in any other form, to any other people, the first say I did not appear to the second, because I did not look to the second as I did to the first, nor say the same things—so how could it have been Me?

You see, then, it matters not in what form or in what manner I reveal Myself—*whatever* manner I choose and *whatever form* I take, *none* will be incontrovertible.

But if You *did* something that would evidence the truth of who You are beyond doubt or question. . .

. . .there are still those who would say, it is of the devil, or simply someone's imagination. Or any cause other than Me.

If I revealed myself as God Almighty, King of Heaven and Earth, and moved mountains to prove it, there are those who would say, "It must have been Satan."

And such is as it should be. For God does not reveal Godself to Godself from or through outward observation, but through inward experience. And when inward experience has revealed Godself, outward observation is not necessary. And if outward observation is necessary, inward experience is not possible.

If, then, revelation is requested, it cannot be had, for the act of asking is a statement that it is not there; that nothing of God is now being revealed. Such a statement produces the experience. For your thought about something is *creative*, and your word is *productive*, and your thought and your word together are magnificently effective in giving birth to your reality. Therefore shall you experience that *God is not now revealed*, for if God *were*, you would not *ask* God to be.

Does that mean I cannot ask for anything I want? Are You saying that praying for something actually *pushes it away from us?*

> This is a question which has been asked through the Ages—and has been answered whenever it has been asked. Yet you have not heard the answer, or will not believe it.
>
> The question is answered again, in today's terms, and today's language, thusly:
>
> You will not have that for which you ask, nor can you have anything you want. This is because your very request is a statement of lack, and your saying you want a thing only works to produce that precise experience—wanting—in your reality.
>
> *The correct prayer is therefore never a prayer of supplication, but a prayer of gratitude.*
>
> When you thank God in *advance* for that which you choose to experience in your reality, you, in effect, acknowledge that it is there. . .*in effect*. Thankfulness is thus the most powerful statement to God; an affirmation that even before you ask, I have answered.
>
> Therefore never supplicate. *Appreciate*.

But what if I am grateful to God in advance for something, and it never shows up? That could lead to disillusionment and bitterness.

> Gratitude cannot be used as a tool with which to *manipulate* God; a *device* with which to fool the universe. You cannot lie to yourself. Your mind knows the truth of your thoughts. If you are saying "Thank you, God, for such and such," all the while being very clear that it isn't *there* in your present reality, you can't expect God to be *less clear* than you, and so produce it for you.
>
> God knows what you know, and what you know is what appears as your reality.

But how then can I be truly grateful for something I *know is not there?*

Faith. If you have but the faith of a mustard seed, you shall move mountains. You come to know it is there because I *said* it is there; because I *said* that, even before you ask, I shall have answered; because I *said,* and have said to you in every conceivable way, through every teacher you can name, that whatsoever you shall choose, choosing it in My Name, so shall it be.

Yet so many people say that their prayers have gone unanswered.

No prayer—and a prayer is nothing more than a fervent statement of *what is so*—goes unanswered. Every prayer—every thought, every statement, every feeling—is creative. To the degree that it is fervently held as truth, to that degree will it be made manifest in your experience.

When it is said that a prayer has not been answered, what has in actuality happened is that the most fervently held thought, word, or feeling has become *operative.* Yet what you must know—and here is the secret—is that always it is the thought behind the thought—what might be called the Sponsoring Thought—that is the controlling thought.

If, therefore, you beg and supplicate, there seems a much smaller chance that you will experience what you think you are choosing, because the Sponsoring Thought behind every supplication is that you do *not have now* what you wish. *That Sponsoring Thought becomes your reality.*

The only Sponsoring Thought which could override this thought is the thought held in faith that God will grant whatever is asked, *without fail.* Some people have such faith, but very few.

The process of prayer becomes much easier when,

rather than having to believe that God will always say "yes" to every request, one understands intuitively that *the request itself is not necessary. Then the prayer is a prayer of thanksgiving. It is not a request at all, but a statement of gratitude for what is so.*

When you say that a prayer is a statement of what is so, are you saying that God does nothing; that everything which happens after a prayer is a result of the *prayer's* action?

If you believe that God is some omnipotent being who hears all prayers, says "yes" to some, "no" to others, and "maybe, but not now" to the rest, you are mistaken. By what rule of thumb would God decide?

If you believe that God is the *creator and decider of all things* in your life, you are mistaken.

God is the *observer*, not the creator. And God stands ready to assist you in living your life, but not in the way you might expect.

It is not God's function to create, or uncreate, the circumstances or conditions of your life. God created *you*, in the image and likeness of God. *You* have created the rest, through the power God has given you. God created the process of life and life itself as you know it. Yet God gave you free choice, to do with life as you will.

In this sense, *your will for you is God's will for you.*

You are living your life the way you are living your life, and *I have no preference in the matter.*

This is the grand illusion in which you have engaged: that God *cares* one way or the other what you do.

I do *not* care what you do, and that is hard for you to hear. Yet do you care what your children do when you send them out to play? Is it a matter of consequence to you whether they play tag, or hide and seek, or pretend? No, it is not, because you know they are perfectly safe. You have placed them in an environment which you consider friendly and very okay.

Of course, you will always hope that they do not

hurt themselves. And if they do, you will be right there to help them, heal them, allow them to feel safe again, to be happy again, to go and play again another day. But whether they choose hide and seek or pretend will not matter to you the next day, either.

You will tell them, of course, which games are dangerous to play. But you cannot stop your children from doing dangerous things. Not always. Not forever. Not in every moment from now until death. It is the wise parent who knows this. Yet the parent never stops caring about the *outcome*. It is this dichotomy—not caring deeply about the process, but caring deeply about the result—that comes close to describing the dichotomy of God.

Yet God, in a sense, does not even care about the outcome. Not the *ultimate outcome*. This is because the ultimate outcome is assured.

And this is the second great illusion of man: that the outcome of life is in doubt.

It is this doubt about ultimate outcome that has created your greatest enemy, which is fear. For if you doubt outcome, then you must doubt Creator—you must *doubt God*. And if you doubt God, you *must* live in fear and guilt all your life.

If you doubt God's intentions—and God's ability to produce this ultimate result—then how can you ever relax? How can you ever truly find peace?

Yet God has *full power* to match intentions with results. You cannot and will not believe in this (even though you claim that God is all-powerful), and so you have to create in your imagination a *power equal to God,* in order that you may find a way for *God's will to be thwarted.* And so you have created in your mythology the being you call "devil." You have even imagined a God at *war* with this being (thinking that God solves problems the way you do). Finally, you have actually imagined that God could *lose* this war.

All of this violates everything you say you know about God, but this doesn't matter. You live your illusion, and thus feel your fear, all out of your decision to doubt God.

But what if you made a new decision? What then would be the result?

I tell you this: you would live as the Buddha did. As Jesus did. As did every saint you have ever idolized.

Yet, as with most of those saints, people would not understand you. And when you tried to explain your sense of peace, your joy in life, your inner ecstasy, they would listen to your words, but not hear them. They would try to repeat your words, but would add to them.

They would wonder how you could have what they cannot find. And then they would grow jealous. Soon jealousy would turn to rage, and in their anger they would try to convince you that it is *you* who do not understand God.

And if they were unsuccessful at tearing you from your joy, they would seek to harm you, so enormous would be their rage. And when you told them it does not matter, that even death cannot interrupt your joy, nor change your truth, they would surely *kill you.* Then, when they saw the peace with which you accepted death, they would call you saint, and love you again.

For it is the nature of people to love, then destroy, then love again that which they value most.

But why? Why do we *do* that?

All human actions are motivated at their deepest level by one of two emotions—fear or love. In truth there are only two emotions—only two words in the language of the soul. These are the opposite ends of the great polarity which I created when I produced the universe, and your world, as you know it today.

These are the two points—the Alpha and the Omega—which allow the system you call "relativity" to be. Without these two points, without these two ideas about things, no other idea could exist.

Every human thought, and every human action, is based in either love or fear. There *is* no other human

15

motivation, and all other ideas are but derivatives of
these two. They are simply different versions—different
twists on the same theme.

Think on this deeply and you will see that it is true.
This is what I have called the Sponsoring Thought. It is
either a thought of love or fear. This is the thought
behind the thought *behind* the thought. It is the first
thought. It is prime force. It is the raw energy that drives
the engine of human experience.

And here is how human behavior produces repeat
experience after repeat experience; it is why humans
love, then destroy, then love again: always there is the
swing from one emotion to the other. Love sponsors
fear sponsors love sponsors fear. . .

. . .And the reason is found in the first lie—the lie
which you hold as the truth about God—that God
cannot be trusted; that God's love cannot be depended
upon; that God's acceptance of you is conditional; that
the ultimate outcome is thus in doubt. For if you cannot
depend on *God's* love to always be there, on whose
love *can* you depend? If God retreats and withdraws
when you do not perform properly, will not mere
mortals also?

. . .*And so it is that in the moment you pledge your
highest love, you greet your greatest fear.*

For the first thing you worry about after saying "I love
you" is whether you'll hear it back. And if you hear it
back, then you begin immediately to worry that the love
you have just found, you will lose. And so all action
becomes a reaction—defense against loss—*even as you
seek to defend yourself against the loss of God.*

Yet if you knew Who You Are—that you are the
most magnificent, the most remarkable, the most splen-
did being God has ever created—you would never fear.
For who could reject such wondrous magnificence? Not
even God could find fault in such a being.

But you do not know Who You Are, and you think
you are a great deal less. And where did you get the
idea of how much less than magnificent you are? From

the only people whose word you would take on *every-thing. From your mother and your father.*

These are the people who love you the most. Why would they lie to you? Yet have they not told you that you are too much of this, and not enough of that? Have they not reminded you that you are to be seen and not heard? Have they not scolded you in some of the moments of your greatest exuberance? And, did they not encourage you to set aside some of your wildest imagining?

These are the messages you've received, and though they do not meet the criteria, and are thus not messages from God, they might as well have been, for they have come from the gods of your universe surely enough.

It was your parents who taught you that love is conditional—you have felt their conditions many times—and that is the experience you take into your own love relationships.

It is also the experience you bring to Me.

From this experience you draw your conclusions about Me. Within this framework you speak your truth. "God is a loving God," you say, "but if you break His commandments, He will punish you with eternal banishment and everlasting damnation."

For have you not experienced the banishment of your own parents? Do you not know the pain of their damnation? How, then, could you imagine it to be any different with Me?

You have forgotten what it was like to be loved without condition. You do not remember the experience of the love of God. And so you try to imagine what God's love must be like, based on what you see of love in the world.

You have projected the role of "parent" onto God, and have thus come up with a God Who judges and rewards or punishes, based on how good He feels about what you've been up to. But this is a simplistic view of God, based on your mythology. It has nothing to do with Who I Am.

Having thus created an entire thought system about God based on human experience rather than spiritual truths, you then create an entire reality around love. It is a fear-based reality, rooted in the idea of a fearful, vengeful God. Its Sponsoring Thought is wrong, but to deny that thought would be to disrupt your whole theology. And though the new theology which would replace it would _truly_ be your salvation, you cannot accept it, _because the idea of a God Who is not to be feared, Who will not judge, and Who has no cause to punish is simply too magnificent to be embraced within even your grandest notion of Who and What God is._

This fear-based love reality dominates your experience of love; indeed, actually creates it. For not only do you see yourself _receiving_ love which is conditional, you also watch yourself _giving_ it in the same way. And even while you withhold and retreat and set your conditions, a part of you knows this is not what love really is. Still, you seem powerless to change the way you dispense it. You've learned the hard way, you tell yourself, and you'll be damned if you're going to leave yourself vulnerable again. Yet the truth is, you'll be damned if you don't.

[By your own (mistaken) thoughts about love do you damn yourself never to experience it purely. So, too, do you damn yourself never to know Me as I really am. Until you do. For you shall not be able to deny Me forever, and the moment will come for our Reconciliation.]

Every action taken by human beings is based in love or fear, not simply those dealing with relationships. Decisions affecting business, industry, politics, religion, the education of your young, the social agenda of your nations, the economic goals of your society, choices involving war, peace, attack, defense, aggression, submission; determinations to covet or give away, to save or to share, to unite or to divide—every single free choice you ever undertake arises out of one of the only two possible thoughts there are: a

18

thought of love or a thought of fear.

Fear is the energy which contracts, closes down, draws in, runs, hides, hoards, harms.

Love is the energy which expands, opens up, sends out, stays, reveals, shares, heals.

Fear wraps our bodies in clothing, love allows us to stand naked. Fear clings to and clutches all that we have, love gives all that we have away. Fear holds close, love holds dear. Fear grasps, love lets go. Fear rankles, love soothes. Fear attacks, love amends.

Every human thought, word, or deed is based in one emotion or the other. You have no choice about this, because there is nothing else from which to choose. But you have free choice about which of these to select.

You make it sound so easy, and yet in the moment of decision fear wins more often than not. Why is that?

You have been taught to live in fear. You have been told about the survival of the fittest and the victory of the strongest and the success of the cleverest. Precious little is said about the glory of the most loving. And so you strive to be the fittest, the strongest, the cleverest—in one way or another—and if you see yourself as something less than this in any situation, you fear loss, for you have been told that to be less is to lose.

And so of course you choose the action fear sponsors, for that is what you have been taught. Yet I teach you this: when you choose the action love sponsors, then will you do more than survive, then will you do more than win, then will you do more than succeed. Then will you experience the full glory of Who You Really Are, and who you can be.

To do this you must turn aside the teachings of your well-meaning, but misinformed, worldly tutors, and *hear the teachings of those whose wisdom comes from another source.*

There are many such teachers among you, as

always there have been, for I will not leave you without those who would show you, teach you, guide you, and remind you of these truths. Yet the greatest reminder is not anyone outside you, but the voice within you. This is the first tool that I use, because it is the most accessible.

The voice within is the loudest voice with which I speak, because it is the closest to you. It is the voice which tells you whether everything *else* is true or false, right or wrong, good or bad as you have defined it. It is the radar that sets the course, steers the ship, guides the journey if you but let it.

It is the voice which tells you right now whether the very words you are reading are words of love or words of fear. By this measure can you determine whether they are words to heed or words to ignore.

You said that when I always choose the action that love sponsors, then I will experience the full glory of who I am and who I can be. Will you expand on this please?

There is only one purpose for all of life, and that is for you and all that lives to experience fullest glory.

Everything else you say, think, or do is attendant to that function. There is nothing else for your soul to do, and nothing else your soul *wants* to do.

The wonder of this purpose is that it is never-ending. An ending is a limitation, and God's purpose is without such a boundary. Should there come a moment in which you experience yourself in your fullest glory, you will in that instant imagine an ever greater glory to fulfill. The more you are, the more you can become, and the more you can become, the more you can yet be.

The deepest secret is that life is not a process of discovery, but a process of creation.

You are not discovering yourself, but creating yourself anew. Seek, therefore, not to find out Who You Are, seek to determine Who You Want to Be.

There are those who say that life is a school, that we are here to learn specific lessons, that once we "graduate" we can go on to larger pursuits, no longer shackled by the body. Is this correct?

It is another part of your mythology, based on human experience.

Life is not a school?

No.

We are not here to learn lessons?

No.

Then why *are* we here?

To remember, and re-create, Who You Are.
I have told you, over and over again. You do not believe Me. Yet that is well as it should be. For truly, if you do not *create* yourself as Who You Are, that you cannot be.

Okay, You've lost me. Let's go back to this school bit. I've heard teacher after teacher tell us that life is a school. I'm frankly shocked to hear You deny that.

School is a place you go if there is something you do not know that you want to know. It is not a place you go if you already know a thing and simply want to *experience your knowingness.*
Life (as you call it) is an opportunity for you to *know experientially* what you already know *conceptually.* You need *learn nothing* to do this. You need merely remember what you already know, and *act on it.*

I'm not sure I understand.

Let's start here. The soul—your soul—knows all there is to know all the time. There's nothing hidden to it, nothing unknown. Yet knowing is not enough. The soul seeks to *experience*.

You can *know* yourself to be generous, but unless you *do* something which displays generosity, you have nothing but a concept. You can *know* yourself to be kind, but unless you *do* someone a kindness, you have nothing but an *idea* about yourself.

It is your soul's only desire to turn its grandest *concept* about itself into its greatest *experience*. Until concept becomes experience, all there is is speculation. I have been speculating about Myself for a long time. Longer than you and I could collectively remember. Longer than the age of this universe times the age of the universe. You see, then, how young is—how *new* is—My experience of Myself!

You've lost me again. Your experience of Yourself?

Yes. Let me explain it to you this way:

In the beginning, that which *Is* is all there was, and there was nothing else. Yet All That Is could not know itself—because All That Is is all there was, and there was *nothing else*. And so, All That Is. . .was *not*. For in the absence of something else, All That Is, is *not*.

This is the great Is/Not Is to which mystics have referred from the beginning of time.

Now All That Is *knew* it was all there was—but this was not enough, for it could only know its utter magnificence *conceptually*, not *experientially*. Yet the *experience* of itself is that for which it longed, for it wanted to know what it felt like to be so magnificent. Still, this was impossible, because the very term "magnificent" is a relative term. All That Is could not know what it *felt* like to be magnificent unless *that which is not* showed up. In the absence of *that which is not*, that which IS, is *not*.

Do you understand this?

I think so. Keep going.

Alright.

The one thing that All That Is knew is that there was *nothing else.* And so It could, and would, *never* know Itself from a reference point outside of Itself. Such a point did not exist. Only one reference point existed, and that was the single place within. The "Is-Not Is." The Am-Not Am.

Still, the All of Everything chose to know Itself *experientially.*

This *energy*—this pure, unseen, unheard, unobserved, and therefore unknown-by-anyone-else energy—chose to experience Itself as the utter magnificence It was. In order to do this, It realized It would have to use a reference point *within.*

It reasoned, quite correctly, that any *portion* of Itself would necessarily have to be *less than the whole,* and that if It thus simply *divided* Itself into portions, each portion, being less than the whole, could look back on the rest of Itself and see magnificence.

And so All That Is divided Itself—becoming, in one glorious moment, that which is *this,* and that which is *that.* For the first time, *this* and *that* existed, quite apart from each other. And still, both existed simultaneously. As did all that was *neither.*

Thus, *three elements* suddenly existed: that which is *here.* That which is *there.* And that which is *neither here nor there*—but which *must exist* for *here* and *there* to exist.

It is the nothing which holds the everything. It is the non-space which holds the space. It is the all which holds the parts.

Can you understand this?

Are you following this?

I think I am, actually. Believe it or not, you have used such a clear illustration that I think I'm actually understanding this.

I'm going to go further. Now this *nothing* which holds the *everything* is what some people call God. Yet that is not accurate, either, for it suggests that there is something God is *not*—namely, everything that is not "nothing." But I am *All Things*—seen and unseen—so this description of Me as the Great Unseen—the No-Thing, or the Space Between, an essentially Eastern mystical definition of God, is no more accurate than the essentially Western practical description of God as all that is seen. Those who believe that God is All That Is *and* All That Is Not, are those whose understanding is correct.

Now in creating that which is "here" and that which is "there," God made it possible for God to know Itself. In the moment of this great explosion from within, God created *relativity*—the greatest gift God ever gave to Itself. Thus, *relationship* is the greatest gift God ever gave to you, a point to be discussed in detail later.

From the No-Thing thus sprang the Everything—a spiritual event entirely consistent, incidentally, with what your scientists call The Big Bang theory.

As the elements of all raced forth, *time* was created, for a thing was first *here*, then it was *there*—and the period it took to *get* from here to there was measurable.

Just as the parts of Itself which are seen began to define themselves, "relative" to each other, so, too, did the parts which are unseen.

God knew that for love to exist—and to know itself as *pure love*—its exact opposite had to exist as well. So God voluntarily created the great polarity—the absolute opposite of love—everything that love is not—what is now called fear. In the moment fear existed, love could exist *as a thing that could be experienced.*

It is this *creation of duality* between love and its opposite which humans refer to in their various mythologies as the *birth of evil*, the fall of Adam, the rebellion of Satan, and so forth.

Just as you have chosen to personify pure love as the character you call God, so have you chosen to personify abject fear as the character you call the devil.

Some on Earth have established rather elaborate mythologies around this event, complete with scenarios of battles and war, angelic soldiers and devilish warriors, the forces of good and evil, of light and dark.

This mythology has been mankind's early attempt to understand, and tell others in a way *they* could understand, a cosmic occurrence *of which the human soul is deeply aware, but of which the mind can barely conceive.*

In rendering the universe as a *divided version of Itself,* God produced, from pure energy, all that now exists—both seen and unseen.

In other words, not only was the physical universe thus created, *but the metaphysical universe as well.* The part of God which forms the second half of the Am/Not Am equation also exploded into an infinite number of units smaller than the whole. These energy units you would call spirits.

In some of your religious mythologies it is stated that "God the Father" had many spirit children. This parallel to the human experiences of life multiplying itself seems to be the only way the masses could be made to hold in reality the idea of the sudden appearance—the sudden existence—of countless spirits in the "Kingdom of Heaven."

In this instance, your mythical tales and stories are not so far from ultimate reality—for the endless spirits comprising the totality of Me *are,* in a cosmic sense, My offspring.

My divine purpose in dividing Me was to create sufficient parts of Me so that I could *know Myself experientially.* There is only one way for the Creator to know Itself experientially as the Creator, and that is to create. And so I gave to each of the countless parts of Me (to all of My spirit children) the *same power to create* which I have as the whole.

This is what your religions mean when they say that you were created in the "image and likeness of God." This doesn't mean, as some have suggested, that our physical bodies look alike (although God can adopt whatever physical form God chooses for a particular purpose). It does mean that our essence is the same. We are composed of the same stuff. We ARE the "same stuff"! With all the same properties and abilities—including the ability to create physical reality out of thin air.

My purpose in creating you, My spiritual offspring, was for Me to know Myself as God. I have no way to do that *save through you*. Thus it can be said (and has been, many times) that My purpose for you is that *you* should know yourself as *Me*.

This seems so amazingly simple, yet it becomes very complex—because there is only one way for you to know yourself as Me, and that is for you *first* to know yourself as *not Me*.

Now try to follow this—fight to keep up—because this gets very subtle here. Are you ready?

I think so.

Good. Remember, you've asked for this explanation. You've waited for it for years. You've asked for it in layman's terms, not theological doctrines or scientific theories.

Yes—I know what I've asked.

And having asked, so shall you receive.

Now, to keep things simple, I'm going to use your children of God mythological model as a basis for discussion, because it is a model with which you are familiar—and in many ways it is not that far off.

So let's go back to how this process of self-knowing must work.

There is one way I could have caused all of My spiritual children to know themselves as parts of Me—and that was simply to tell them. This I did. But you see, it was not enough for Spirit to simply know Itself as God, or part of God, or children of God, or inheritors of the kingdom (or whatever mythology you want to use).

As I've already explained, knowing something, and *experiencing* it, are two different things. Spirit longed to know Itself experientially (just as *I* did!). Conceptual awareness was not enough for you. So I devised a plan. It is the most extraordinary idea in all the universe—and the most spectacular collaboration. I say collaboration because *all of you are in it with Me.*

Under the plan, you as pure spirit would enter the physical universe just created. This is because *physicality* is the only way to know experientially what you know conceptually. It is, in fact, the reason I created the physical cosmos to begin with—and the system of relativity which governs it, and all creation.

Once in the physical universe, you, My spirit children, could experience what you know of yourself—but first, you had to *come to know the opposite.* To explain this simplistically, you cannot know yourself as tall unless and until you become aware of short. You cannot experience the part of yourself that you call fat unless you also come to know thin.

Taken to ultimate logic, you cannot experience yourself as what you are until you've encountered what you are *not.* This is the purpose of the theory of relativity, and all physical life. It is by that which you are *not* that you yourself are defined.

Now in the case of the ultimate knowing—in the case of knowing yourself as the Creator—you cannot *experience* your Self as creator unless and until you *create.* And you cannot create yourself until you *un-create* yourself. In a sense, you have to first "not be" in order to be. Do you follow?

I think. . .

Stay with it.

Of course, there is no way for you to not be who and what you are—you simply *are* that (pure, creative spirit), have been always, and always will be. So, you did the next best thing. You *caused yourself to forget* Who You Really Are.

Upon entering the physical universe, you *relinquished your remembrance of yourself.* This allows you to *choose* to be Who You Are, rather than simply wake up in the castle, so to speak.

It is in the act of choosing to be, rather than simply being told that you are, a part of God that you *experience* yourself as being at total choice, which is what, by definition, God is. Yet how can you have a choice about something over which there *is* no choice? You cannot *not* be My offspring no matter how hard you try—but you *can forget.*

You are, have always been, and will always be, a *divine part* of the *divine whole,* a *member of the body.* That is why the act of rejoining the whole, of returning to God, is called *remembrance.* You actually choose to *re-member* Who You Really Are, or to join together with the various parts of you to experience the all of you—which is to say, the All of *Me.*

Your job on Earth, therefore, is not to *learn* (because you *already know*), but to *re-member* Who You Are. And to re-member who everyone else is. That is why a big part of your job is to remind others (that is, to *re-mind* them), so that they can re-member also.

All the wonderful spiritual teachers have been doing just that. It is *your* sole purpose. That is to say, your *soul purpose.*

My God, this is so simple—and so. . .*symmetrical.* I mean, it all fits *in!* It all suddenly *fits!* I see, now, a picture I have never quite put together before.

Good. That is good. That is the purpose of this

dialogue. You have asked Me for answers. I have promised I would give them to you.

*You will make of this dialogue a book, and you will
render My words accessible to many people. It is part of
your work.* Now, you have many questions, many
inquiries to make about life. We have here placed the
foundation. We have laid the groundwork for other
understandings. Let us go to these other questions. And
do not worry. If there is something about what we've
just gone through you do not thoroughly understand, it
will all be clear to you soon enough.

There is so much I want to ask. There are so many questions.
I suppose I should start with the big ones, the obvious ones.
Like, why is the world in the shape it's in?

Of all the questions man has asked of God, this is
the one asked most often. From the beginning of time
man has asked it. From the first moment to this you have
wanted to know, *why must it be like this?*

The classic posing of the question is usually something like: If God is all-perfect and all-loving, why would
God create pestilence and famine, war and disease,
earthquakes and tornados and hurricanes and all manner of natural disaster, deep personal disappointment,
and worldwide calamity?

The answer to this question lies in the deeper mystery of the universe and the highest meaning of life.

*I do not show My goodness by creating only what
you call perfection all around you. I do not demonstrate
My love by not allowing you to demonstrate yours.*

As I have already explained, you cannot demonstrate love until you can demonstrate *not* loving. A thing
cannot exist without its opposite, except in the world
of the absolute. Yet the realm of the absolute was not
sufficient for either you or Me. I existed there, in the
always, and it is from where you, too, have come.

In the absolute there is no experience, only knowing.

Knowing is a divine state, yet the grandest joy is in being. *Being* is achieved only after experience. The evolution is this: *knowing, experiencing, being*. This is the Holy Trinity—the Triune that is God.

God the Father is *knowing*—the parent of all understandings, the begetter of all experience, for you cannot experience that which you do not know.

God the Son is *experiencing*—the embodiment, the acting out, of all that the Father knows of Itself, for you cannot be that which you have not experienced.

God the Holy Spirit is *being*—the *dis*embodiment of all that the Son has experienced of Itself; the simple, exquisite is-ness possible only through the memory of the knowing and experiencing.

This simple being is bliss. It is God-state, after knowing and experiencing Itself. It is that for which God yearned in the beginning.

Of course, you are well past the point where you must have it explained to you that the father-son descriptions of God have nothing to do with gender. I use here the picturesque speech of your most recent scriptures. Much earlier holy writings placed this metaphor in a mother-daughter context. Neither is correct. Your mind can best hold the relationship as: parent-offspring. Or: that-which-gives-rise-to, and that-which-is-risen.

Adding the third part of the Trinity produces this relationship:

That which gives rise to / That which is risen / That which is.

This Triune Reality is God's signature. It is the divine pattern. The three-in-one is everywhere found in the realms of the sublime. You cannot escape it in matters dealing with time and space, God and consciousness, or any of the subtle relationships. On the other hand, you will *not* find the Triune Truth in any of life's gross relationships.

The Triune Truth is recognized in life's subtle relationships by everyone dealing with such relationships. Some of your religionists have described the Triune

Truth as Father, Son, and Holy Ghost. Some of your psychiatrists use the terms superconscious, conscious and subconscious. Some of your spiritualists say mind, body, and spirit. Some of your scientists see energy, matter, ether. Some of your philosophers say a thing is not true for you until it is true in thought, word, and deed. When discussing time, you speak of three times only: past, present, future. Similarly, there are three moments in your perception—before, now, and after. In terms of spatial relationships, whether considering the points in the universe, or various points in your own room, you recognize here, there, and the space in between.

In matters of gross relationships, you recognize _no_ "in-between." That is because gross relationships are always dyads, whereas relationships of the higher realm are invariably triads. Hence, there is left-right, up-down, big-small, fast-slow, hot-cold, and the greatest dyad ever created: male-female. There are no _in-betweens_ in these dyads. A thing is either _one thing or the other_, or some greater or lesser _version_ in relationship _to_ one of these polarities.

Within the realm of gross relationships, nothing conceptualized can exist without a conceptualization of its _opposite_. Most of your day-to-day experience is foundationed in this reality.

Within the realm of sublime relationships nothing which exists _has_ an opposite. All Is One, and everything progresses from one to the other in a never-ending circle.

Time is such a sublime realm, in which what you call past, present, and future exist _inter-relationally_. That is, they are not _opposites_, but rather parts of the same whole; progressions of the same idea; cycles of the same energy; aspects of the same immutable Truth. If you conclude from this that past, present, and future exist at one and the same "time," you are right. (Yet now is not the moment to discuss that. We can get into this in much greater detail when we explore the whole concept of time—which we will do later.)

The world is the way it is because it could not be any *other* way and still exist in the gross realm of physicality. Earthquakes and hurricanes, floods and tornados, and events that you call natural disasters are but movements of the elements from one polarity to the other. The whole birth-death cycle is part of this movement. These are the rhythms of life, and everything in gross reality is subject to them, because life *itself* is a rhythm. It is a wave, a vibration, a pulsation at the very heart of the All That Is.

Illness and disease are opposites of health and wellness, and are made manifest in your reality at your behest. You cannot be ill without at some level causing yourself to be, and you can be well again in a moment by simply deciding to be. Deep personal disappointments are responses which are chosen, and worldwide calamities are the result of worldwide consciousness.

Your question infers that I choose these events, that it is My will and *desire* they should occur. *Yet I do not will these things into being, I merely observe* you *doing so.* And I do nothing to stop them, because to do so would be to *thwart your will.* That, in turn, would deprive you of the God experience, which is the experience you and I have chosen together.

Do not condemn, therefore, all that you would call bad in the world. Rather, ask yourself, what about this have you judged bad, and what, if anything, you wish to do to change it.

Inquire within, rather than without, asking: "What part of my Self do I wish to experience now in the face of this calamity? What aspect of being do I choose to call forth?" For all of life exists as a tool of your own creation, and all of its events merely present themselves as opportunities for you to decide, and be, Who You Are.

This is true for *every* soul, and so you see there are no victims in the universe, only creators. The Masters who have walked this planet all knew this. That is why, no matter which Master you might name, none imagined themselves to be victimized—though many were truly crucified.

Each soul is a Master—though some do not remember their origins or their heritages. Yet each creates the situation and the circumstance for its own highest purpose and its own quickest remembering—in each moment called now.

Judge not, then, the karmic path walked by another. *Envy not success, nor pity failure, for you know not what is success or failure in the soul's reckoning.* Call not a thing calamity, nor joyous event, until you decide, or witness, how it is *used.* For is a death a calamity if it saves the lives of thousands? And is a life a joyous event if it has caused nothing but grief? Yet even this you should not judge, but keep always your own counsel, and allow others theirs.

This does not mean ignore a call for help, nor the urging of your own soul to work toward the change of some circumstance or condition. It does mean avoiding labels and judgment while you do whatever you do. For each circumstance is a gift, and in each experience is hidden a treasure.

There once was a soul who knew itself to be the light. This was a new soul, and so, anxious for experience. "I am the light," it said. "I am the light." Yet all the knowing of it and all the saying of it could not substitute for the experience of it. And in the realm from which this soul emerged, there was nothing *but* the light. *Every* soul was grand, every soul was magnificent, and every soul shone with the brilliance of My awesome light. And so the little soul in question was as a candle in the sun. In the midst of the grandest light—of which it was a part—it could not see itself, nor experience itself as Who and What it Really Is.

Now it came to pass that this soul yearned and yearned to know itself. And so great was its yearning that I one day said, "Do you know, Little One, what you must do to satisfy this yearning of yours?"

"Oh, what, God? What? I'll do *anything!*" The little soul said.

"You must separate yourself from the rest of us," I answered, "and then you must call upon yourself the darkness."

"What is the darkness, o Holy One?" the little soul asked.

"That which you are not," I replied, and the soul understood.

And so this the soul did, removing itself from the All, yea, going even unto another realm. And in this realm the soul had the power to call into its experience all sorts of darkness. And this it did.

Yet in the midst of all the darkness did it cry out, "Father, Father, why hast Thou forsaken me?" Even as have you in your blackest times. Yet I have never forsaken you, but stand by you always, ready to remind you of Who You Really Are; ready, always ready, to call you home.

Therefore, be a light unto the darkness, and curse it not.

And forget not Who You Are in the moment of your encirclement by that which you are not. But do you praise to the creation, even as you seek to change it.

And know that what you do in the time of your greatest trial can be your greatest triumph. For the experience you create is a statement of Who You Are—and Who You Want to Be.

I have told you this story—the parable of the little soul and the sun—so that you might better understand why the world is the way it is—and how it can change in an instant the moment everyone remembers the divine truth of their highest reality.

Now there are those who say that life is a school, and that these things which you observe and experience in your life are for your learning. I have addressed this before, and I tell you again:

You came into this life with nothing to learn—you have only to demonstrate what you already know. In the demonstration of it will you function it out, and create yourself anew, through your experience. Thus do you justify life, and give it purpose. Thus do you render it holy.

Are you saying that all the bad things that happen to us are things of our own choosing? Do you mean that even the world's calamities and disasters are, at some level, created by us so that we can "experience the opposite of Who We Are"? And, if so, isn't there some less painful way—less painful to ourselves and others—to create opportunities for us to experience ourselves?

You've asked several questions, and they are all good ones. Let's take them one at a time.

No, not all the things which you call bad which happen to you are of your own choosing. Not in the conscious sense—which you mean. They *are* all of your own *creation*.

You are *always* in the process of *creating*. Every moment. Every minute. Every day. *How* you can create we'll go into later. For now, just take my word for it—you are a big creation machine, and you are turning out a new manifestation literally as fast as you can think.

Events, occurrences, happenings, conditions, circumstances—all are created out of consciousness. Individual consciousness is powerful enough. You can imagine what kind of creative energy is unleashed whenever two or *more* are gathered in My name. And *mass* consciousness? Why, *that* is so powerful it can create events and circumstances of worldwide import and planetary consequences.

It would not be accurate to say—not in the way *you* mean it—that *you* are *choosing* these consequences. You are not choosing them anymore than I am choosing them. Like Me, you are observing them. And deciding Who You Are *with regard to them*.

Yet there are no victims in the world, and no villains. And neither are you a victim of the choices of others.

At some level you have _all_ created that which you say you detest—and, having created it, you have _chosen_ it.

This is an advanced level of thinking, and it is one which all Masters reach sooner or later. For it is only when they can accept responsibility for _all_ of it that they can achieve the power to change _part_ of it.

So long as you entertain the notion that there is something or someone else out there "doing it" to you, you disempower yourself to do anything about it. Only when you say "I _did_ this" can you find the power to change it.

It is much easier to change what you are doing than to change what another is doing.

The first step in changing _anything_ is to know and accept that you have chosen it to be what it is. If you can't accept this on a personal level, agree to it through your understanding that We are all One. Seek then to create change not because a thing is wrong, but because it no longer makes an accurate statement of Who You Are.

There is only one reason to do anything: as a statement to the universe of Who You Are.

Used in this way, life becomes Self creative. You use life to create your _Self_ as Who You Are, and Who You've Always Wanted to _Be_. There is also only one reason to _un_-do anything: because it is _no longer_ a statement of Who You Want to Be. It does not reflect you. It does not represent you. (That is, it does not re-_present_ you. . .)

If you wish to be accurately re-presented, _you must work to change anything in your life which does not fit into the picture of you that you wish to project into eternity._

In the largest sense, all the "bad" things that happen _are_ of your choosing. The mistake is not in choosing them, but in calling them bad. For in calling them bad, you call your Self bad, since you created them.

This label you cannot accept, so rather than label your Self bad, you _disown your own creations_. It is this intellectual and spiritual dishonesty which lets you accept a world in which conditions are as they are. If you had to accept—or even felt a deep inner sense of—*personal responsibility* for the world, it would be a far different place. This would *certainly* be true if *everyone* felt responsible. That this is so patently obvious is what makes it so utterly painful, and so poignantly ironic.

The world's natural calamities and disasters—its tornados and hurricanes, volcanoes and floods—its physical turmoils—are not created by you specifically. What *is* created by you is the degree to which these events touch your life.

Events occur in the universe which no stretch of the imagination could claim you instigated or created.

These events are created by the combined consciousness of man. All of the world, co-creating together, produces these experiences. What each of you do, individually, is move through them, deciding what, if anything, they mean to you, and Who and What You Are in relationship to them.

Thus, you create collectively, and individually, the life and times you are experiencing, for the soul purpose of evolving.

You've asked if there is a less painful way to undergo this process—and the answer is yes—yet nothing in your outward experience will have changed. The way to reduce the pain which you associate with earthly experiences and events—both yours and those of others—is *to change the way you behold them.*

You cannot change the outer event (for that has been created by the lot of you, and you are not grown enough in your consciousness to alter individually that which has been created collectively), so you must change the inner experience. This is the road to mastery in living.

Nothing is painful in and of itself. Pain is a result of wrong thought. It is an error in thinking.

A Master can disappear the most grievous pain. In this way, the Master heals.

Pain results from a judgment you have made about a thing. Remove the judgment and the pain disappears.

Judgment is often based upon previous experience. Your idea about a thing derives from a prior idea about that thing. Your prior idea results from a still prior idea—and that idea from another, and so forth, like building blocks, until you get all the way back in the hall of mirrors to what I call first thought.

All thought is creative, and no thought is more powerful than original thought. That is why this is sometimes also called original sin.

Original sin is when your first thought about a thing is in error. That error is compounded many times over when you have a second or third thought about a thing. It is the job of the Holy Spirit to inspire you to new understandings, which can free you from your mistakes.

Are you saying that I shouldn't feel bad about the starving children of Africa, the violence and injustice in America, the earthquake that kills hundreds in Brazil?

There are no "shoulds" or "shouldn'ts" in God's world. Do what you want to do. Do what reflects you, what re-presents you as a grander version of your Self. If you want to feel bad, feel bad.

But judge not, and neither condemn, for you know not why a thing occurs, nor to what end.

And remember you this: that which you condemn will condemn you, and that which you judge, you will one day become.

Rather, seek to change those things—or support others who are changing those things—which no longer reflect your highest sense of Who You Are.

Yet, bless all—for all is the creation of God, through life living, and that is the highest creation.

Could we just stop here for a moment and let me catch my breath? Did I hear you say there are no "shoulds" or "should nots" in God's world?

That is correct.

How can that be? If there are none in *Your* world, where *would* they be?

Indeed—where. . .?

I repeat the question. Where else would "shoulds" and "should nots" appear, if not in Your world?

In your *imagination*.

But those who have taught me all about the rights and wrongs, the dos and don'ts, the shoulds and shouldn'ts, told me all those rules were laid down by *You*—by God.

Then those who taught you were wrong. I have never set down a "right" or "wrong," a "do" or a "don't." To do so would be to strip you completely of your greatest gift—the opportunity to do as you please, and experience the results of that; the chance to create yourself anew in the image and likeness of Who You Really Are; the space to produce a reality of a higher and higher you, based on your grandest idea of what it is of which you are capable.

To *say* that something—a thought, a word, an action—is "wrong" would be as much as to tell you not to do it. To tell you not to do it would be to prohibit you. To prohibit you would be to restrict you. To restrict you would be to deny the reality of Who You Really Are, as well as the opportunity for you to create and experience that truth.

There are those who say that I have given you free will, yet these same people claim that if you do not obey Me, I will send you to hell. What kind of free will is that? Does this not make a mockery of God—to say nothing of any sort of true relationship between us?

39

Well, now we're getting into another area I wanted to discuss, and that's this whole business about heaven and hell. From what I'm gathering here, there is no such thing as hell.

There is hell, but it is not what you think, and you do not experience it for the reasons you have been given.

What is hell?

It is the experience of the worst possible outcome of your choices, decisions, and creations. It is the natural consequence of any thought which denies Me, or says no to Who You Are in relationship to Me.

It is the pain you suffer through wrong thinking. Yet even the term "wrong thinking" is a misnomer, because there is no such thing as that which is wrong.

Hell is the opposite of joy. It is unfulfillment. It is knowing Who and What You Are, and failing to experience that. It is being *less*. That is hell, and there is none greater for your soul.

But hell does not exist as this *place* you have fantasized, where you burn in some everlasting fire, or exist in some state of everlasting torment. What purpose could I have in that?

Even if I did hold the extraordinarily unGodly thought that you did not "deserve" heaven, why would I have a need to seek some kind of revenge, or punishment, for your failing? Wouldn't it be a simple matter for Me to just dispose of you? What vengeful part of Me would require that I subject you to eternal suffering of a type and at a level beyond description?

If you answer, the need for justice, would not a simple denial of communion with Me in heaven serve the ends of justice? Is the unending infliction of pain also required?

I tell you there *is* no such experience after death as

you have constructed in your fear-based theologies. Yet there is an experience of the soul so unhappy, so incomplete, so less than whole, so *separated* from God's greatest joy, that to your soul this would *be* hell. But I tell you I do not *send* you there, nor do I cause this experience to be visited upon you. You, yourself, create the experience, whenever and however you separate your Self from your own highest thought about you. You, yourself, create the experience, whenever you deny your Self; whenever you reject Who and What You Really Are.

Yet even this experience is never eternal. It *cannot* be, for it is not My plan that you shall be separated from Me forever and ever. Indeed, such a thing is an impossibility—for to achieve such an event, not only would *you* have to deny Who You Are—I would have to as well. This I will never do. And so long as one of us holds the truth about you, the truth about you shall ultimately prevail.

But if there is no hell, does that mean I can do what I want, act as I wish, commit any act, without fear of retribution?

Is it *fear* that you need in order to be, do, and have what is intrinsically right? Must you be *threatened* in order to "be good"? And what is "being good"? Who gets to have the final say about that? Who sets the guidelines? Who makes the rules?

I tell you this: *You* are your own rule-maker. You set the guidelines. And *you* decide how well you have done; how well you are doing. For *you* are the one who has decided Who and What You Really Are—and Who You Want to Be. And *you* are the *only one* who can assess how well you're doing.

No one else will judge you ever, for why, and how, could God judge God's own creation and call it bad? If I wanted you to be and do everything perfectly, I would have left you in the state of total perfection whence you came. The whole point of the process was for you to discover yourself, *create* your Self, as you truly are—and as you truly wish to be. Yet you could not be that unless you also had a choice to *be something else.*

Should I therefore punish you for making a choice that I Myself have laid before you? If I did not want you to make the second choice, why would I create other than the first?

This is a question you must ask yourself before you would assign Me the role of a condemning God.

The direct answer to your question is, yes, you may do as you wish without fear of retribution. It may serve you, however, to be aware of consequences.

Consequences are results. Natural outcomes. These are not at all the same as retributions, or punishments. Outcomes are simply that. They are what results from the natural application of natural laws. They are that *which* occurs, quite predictably, as a consequence of what *has* occurred.

All physical life functions in accordance with natural laws. Once you remember these laws, and apply them, you have mastered life at the physical level.

What seems like punishment to you—or what you would call evil, or bad luck—is nothing more than a natural law asserting itself.

Then if I were to know these laws, and obey them, I would never have a moment's trouble again. Is that what you're telling me?

You would never experience your Self as being in what you call "trouble." You would not understand any life situation to be a problem. You would not encounter any circumstance with trepidation. You would put an end to all worry, doubt, and fear. You would live as you fantasize Adam and Eve lived—not as disembodied spirits in the realm of the absolute, but as embodied spirits in the realm of the relative. Yet you would have all the freedom, all the joy, all the peace, and all the wisdom, understanding and power of the Spirit you are. You would be a fully realized being.

This is the goal of your soul. This is its purpose—to fully realize itself while in the body; to become the _embodiment_ of all that it really is.

This is My plan for you. This is My ideal: that I should become realized through you. That thus, concept is turned into experience, that I might know my Self _experientially._

The Laws of the Universe are laws that I laid down. They are perfect laws, creating perfect function of the physical.

Have you ever seen anything more perfect than a snowflake? Its intricacy, its design, its symmetry, its conformity to itself and originality from all else—all are a mystery. You wonder at the miracle of this awesome display of Nature. Yet if I can do this with a single snowflake, what think you I can do—have _done_—with the universe?

Were you to see the symmetry of it, the perfection of its design—from the largest body to the smallest particle—you would not be able to hold the truth of it in your reality. Even now, as you get glimpses of it, you cannot yet imagine or understand its implications. Yet you can know there _are_ implications—far more complex and far more extraordinary than your present comprehension can embrace. Your Shakespeare said it wonderfully: _There are more things in Heaven and Earth, Horatio, than are dreamt of in your philosophy._

Then how can I know these laws? How can I learn them?

It is not a question of learning, but of remembering.

How can I remember them?

Begin by being still. Quiet the outer world, so that the inner world might bring you sight. This in-*sight* is what you seek, yet you cannot have it while you are so deeply concerned with your outer reality. Seek, therefore, to go within as much as possible. And when you are not going within, come *from* within as you deal with the outside world. Remember this axiom:

If you do not go within, you go without.

Put it in the first person as you repeat it, to make it more personal:

> If I do not
> go within
> I
> *go without*

You have been going without all your life. Yet you do not have to, and never did.

There is nothing you cannot be, there is nothing you cannot do. There is nothing you cannot have.

That sounds like a pie-in-the-sky promise.

What other kind of promise would you have God make? Would you believe Me if I promised you less?

For thousands of years people have disbelieved the promises of God for the most extraordinary reason: they were too good to be true. So you have chosen a lesser promise—a lesser love. For the highest promise of God proceeds from the highest love. Yet you cannot conceive of a perfect love, and so a perfect promise is also inconceivable. As is a perfect person. Therefore you cannot believe even in your Self.

Failing to believe in any of this means failure to believe in God. For belief in God produces belief in God's greatest gift—unconditional love—and God's greatest promise—unlimited potential.

May I interrupt you here? I hate to interrupt God when He's on a roll...but I've heard this talk of unlimited potential before, and it doesn't square with the human experience. Forget the difficulties encountered by the average person—what about the challenges of those born with mental or physical limitations? Is *their* potential unlimited?

> You have written so in your own Scripture—in many ways and in many places.

Give me one reference.

> Look to see what you have written in Genesis, chapter 11, verse 6, of your Bible.

It says, "And the Lord said, 'Behold, the people are one, and they have all one language; and this is only the beginning of what they will do: and now nothing will be restrained from them, which they have imagined to do.' "

> Yes. Now, can you trust that?

That does not answer the question of the feeble, the infirm, the handicapped, those who are limited.

> Do you think they are limited, as you put it, not of their choice? Do you imagine that a human soul encounters life challenges—*whatever* they may be—by *accident*? Is *this* your imagining?

Do you mean a soul chooses what kind of life it will experience ahead of time?

> No, that would defeat the *purpose* of the encounter. The purpose is to *create* your experience—and thus, create your *Self*—in the glorious moment of Now. You do not, therefore, choose the life you will experience ahead of time.

You may, however, select the persons, places, and events—the conditions and circumstances, the challenges and obstacles, the opportunities and options—with which to *create* your experience. You may select the colors for your palette, the tools for your chest, the machinery for your shop. What you create with these is your business. That *is* the business of life.

Your potential *is* unlimited in all that you've chosen to do. Do not assume that a soul which has incarnated in a body which you call limited has not reached its full potential, for you do not know what that soul was *trying to do*. You do not understand its *agenda*. You are unclear as to its *intent*.

Therefore *bless every* person and condition, and give thanks. Thus you affirm the perfection of God's creation—and show your faith in it. For nothing happens by accident in God's world, and there is no such thing as coincidence. Nor is the world buffeted by random choice, or something you call fate.

If a snowflake is utterly perfect in its design, do you not think the same could be said about something as magnificent as your life?

But even Jesus healed the sick. Why would he heal them if their condition was so "perfect"?

Jesus did not heal those he healed because he saw their condition as imperfect. He healed those he healed because he saw those souls asking for healing as part of their process. He saw the perfection of the process. He recognized and understood the soul's intention. Had Jesus felt that all illness, mental or physical, represented imperfection, would he not have simply healed everyone on the planet, all at once? Do you doubt that he could do this?

No. I believe he could have.

Good. Then the mind begs to know: Why did he not do it? Why would the Christ choose to have some suffer, and others be healed? For that matter, why does God allow any suffering at anytime? This question has been asked before, and the answer remains the same. There is perfection in the process—and all life arises out of *choice*. It is not appropriate to interfere with choice, nor to question it. It is particularly inappropriate to condemn it.

What *is* appropriate is to observe it, and then to do whatever might be done to assist the soul in seeking and making a *higher choice*. Be watchful, therefore, of the choices of others, but not judgmental. Know that their choice is perfect for them in this moment now—yet stand ready to assist them should the moment come when they seek a newer choice, a different choice—a higher choice.

Move into communion with the souls of others, and their purpose, their intention, will be clear to you. This is what Jesus did with those he healed—and with *all* those whose lives he touched. Jesus healed all those who came to him, or who sent others to him supplicating for them. He did not perform a random healing. To have done so would have been to violate a sacred Law of the Universe:

Allow each soul to walk its path.

But does that mean we must not help anyone without being asked? Surely not, or we would never be able to help the starving children of India, or the tortured masses of Africa, or the poor, or the downtrodden anywhere. All humanitarian effort would be lost, all charity forbidden. Must we wait for an individual to cry out to us in desperation, or for a nation of people to plead for help, before we are allowed to do what is obviously right?

You see, the question answers itself. If a thing is obviously right, do it. But remember to exercise extreme judgment regarding what you call "right" and "wrong."

*A thing is only right or wrong because you say it is.
A thing is not right or wrong intrinsically.*

It isn't?

"Rightness" or "wrongness" is not an intrinsic condition, it is a subjective judgment in a personal value
system. By your subjective judgments do you create
your Self—by your personal values do you determine
and demonstrate Who You Are.

The world exists exactly as it is so that you may make
these judgments. If the world existed in perfect condition, your life process of Self creation would be termi-
nated. It would end. A lawyer's career would end
tomorrow were there no more litigation. A doctor's
career would end tomorrow were there no more illness.
A philosopher's career would end tomorrow were there
no more questions.

And *God's career* would end tomorrow were there *no more
problems!*

Precisely. You have put it perfectly. We, all of us,
would be through creating were there nothing more to
create. We, all of us, have a vested interest in *keeping
the game going.* Much as we all say we would like to
solve all the problems, we dare not solve *all* the problems, or there will be nothing left for us to *do.*

Your industrial-military complex understands this
very well. That is why it opposes mightily any attempt
to install a war-no-more government—anywhere.

Your medical establishment understands this, too.
That is why it staunchly opposes—it *must,* it *has to* for
its own survival—any new miracle drug or cure—to say
nothing of the possibility of miracles themselves.

Your religious community also holds this clarity. That
is why it attacks uniformly any definition of God which
does not include fear, judgment and retribution, and

any definition of Self which does not include *their own idea of the only path to God.*

If I say to you, you *are* God—where does that leave religion? If I say to you, you *are* healed, where does that leave science, and medicine? If I say to you, you shall live in peace, where does that leave the peacemakers? If I say to you, the world is fixed—where does that leave the world?

What, now, of plumbers?

The world is filled with essentially two kinds of people: those who give you things you want, and those who fix things. In a sense, even those who simply give you things you want—the butchers, the bakers, the candlestick makers—are also fixers. For to have a desire for something is often to have a *need* for it. That is why addicts are said to need a *fix.* Be careful, therefore, that desire not become *addiction.*

Are you saying the world will always have problems? Are you saying that you actually *want it that way?*

I am saying that the world exists the way it exists—just as a snowflake exists the way it exists—quite by design. *You* have created it that way—just as you have created your life exactly as it is.

I want what *you* want. The day you really want an end to hunger, there will be no more hunger. I have given you all the resources with which to do that. You have all the tools with which to make that choice. You have not made it. Not because you *cannot* make it. The world could end world hunger tomorrow. You *choose* not to make it.

You claim that there are good reasons that 40,000 people a day must die of hunger. There are no good reasons. Yet at a time when you say you can do nothing to stop 40,000 people a day from dying of hunger, you bring 50,000 people a day into your world to begin a new life. And this you call love. This you call God's plan. It is a plan which totally lacks logic or reason, to say nothing of compassion.

I am showing you in stark terms that the world exists the way it exists because *you have chosen for it to*. You are systematically destroying your own environment, then pointing to so-called natural disasters as evidence of God's cruel hoax, or Nature's harsh ways. You have played the hoax on yourself, and it is your ways which are cruel.

Nothing, *nothing* is more gentle than Nature. And nothing, *nothing* has been more cruel to Nature than man. Yet you step aside from all involvement in this; deny all responsibility. It is not your fault, you say, and in this you are right. It is not a question of *fault*, it is a matter of *choice*.

You can choose to end the destruction of your rain forests tomorrow. You can choose to stop depleting the protective layer hovering over your planet. You can *choose* to discontinue the ongoing onslaught of your earth's ingenious ecosystem. You can seek to put the snowflake back together—or at least to halt its inexorable melting—but will you do it?—

You can similarly *end all war tomorrow*. Simply. Easily. All it takes—all it has *ever* taken—is for all of you to agree. Yet if *you* cannot all agree on something as basically simple as ending the killing of each other, how can you call upon the heavens with shaking fist to put your life in order?

I will do nothing for you that you will not do for your Self. *That* is the law and the prophets.

The world is in the condition it is in because of *you*, and the choices you have made—or failed to make.

(Not to decide is to decide.)

The Earth is in the shape it's in because of *you*, and the choices you have made—or failed to make.

Your own life is the way it is because of *you*, and the choices you have made—or failed to make.

But I did not choose to get hit by that truck! I did not choose to get mugged by that robber, or raped by that maniac. People could say that. There are people in the world who could say that.

You are _all_ at root cause for the conditions which exist which create in the robber the desire, or the perceived need, to steal. You have all created the consciousness which makes rape possible. It is when you _see in yourself_ that which caused the crime that you begin, at last, to heal the condition from which it sprang.

Feed your hungry, give dignity to your poor. Grant opportunity to your less fortunate. End the prejudice which keeps masses huddled and angry, with little promise of a better tomorrow. Put away your pointless taboos and restrictions upon sexual energy—rather, help others to truly understand its wonder, and to channel it properly. Do _these_ things and you will go a long way toward ending robbery and rape forever.

As for the so-called "accident"—the truck coming around the bend, the brick falling from the sky—learn to greet each such incident as a small part of a larger mosaic. You have come here to work out an individual plan for your own salvation. Yet salvation does not mean saving yourself from the snares of the devil. There is no such thing as the devil, and hell does not exist. You are saving yourself from the oblivion of non-realization.

You cannot lose in this battle. You cannot fail. Thus it is not a battle at all, but simply a process. Yet if you do not know this, you will see it as a constant struggle. You may even _believe in the struggle_ long enough to create a whole religion around it. This religion will teach that _struggle is the point of it all._ This is a false teaching. It is in _not_ struggling that the process proceeds. It is in surrendering that the victory is won.

Accidents happen because they do. Certain elements of the life process have come together in a particular way at a particular time, with particular results—results which you choose to call unfortunate, for your own particular reasons. Yet they may not be unfortunate at all, given the agenda of your soul.

I tell you this: There _is_ no coincidence, and _nothing_

happens "by accident." Each event and adventure is called *to* your Self *by* your Self in order that you might create and experience Who You Really Are. All true Masters know this. That is why mystic Masters remain unperturbed in the face of the worst experiences of life (as *you* would define them).

The great teachers of your Christian religion understand this. They know that Jesus was not perturbed by the crucifixion, but expected it. He could have walked away, but he did not. He could have stopped the process at any point. He had that power. Yet he did not. He *allowed himself to be crucified* in order that he might stand as man's eternal salvation. *Look,* he said, *at what I can do.* Look at what is *true.* And know that these things, and more, shall you also do. For have I not said, ye are gods? Yet you do not believe. If you cannot, then, believe in your*self*, believe in *me.*

Such was Jesus' compassion that he begged for a way—and created it—to so impact the world that all might come to heaven (Self realization)—if in no other way, then through *him.* For he defeated misery, and death. And so might you.

The grandest teaching of Christ was not that you *shall* have everlasting life—but that you *do*; not that you *shall* have brotherhood in God, but that you *do*; not that you *shall* have whatever you request, but that you *do.*

All that is required is to *know this.* For you *are* the creator of your reality, and life can show up no other way for you than that way in which you *think* it will.

You *think* it into being. This is the first step in creation. God the Father is thought. Your thought is the parent which gives birth to all things.

This is one of the laws we are to remember.

Yes.

Can you tell me others?

I have told you others. I've told you them all, since the beginning of time. Over and over have I told you them. Teacher after teacher have I sent you. You do not listen to my teachers. You kill them.

But *why?* Why do we kill the holiest among us? We kill them or dishonor them, which is the same thing. *Why?*

Because they stand against every thought you have that would deny Me. And deny Me you must if you are to deny your Self.

Why would I want to deny You, *or me?*

Because you are afraid. And because My promises are too good to be true. Because you cannot accept the grandest Truth. And so you must reduce yourself to a spirituality which teaches fear and dependence and intolerance, rather than love and power and acceptance.

You are *filled* with fear—and your biggest fear is that My biggest promise might be life's biggest lie. And so you create the biggest fantasy you can to defend yourself against this: You claim that any promise which gives you the power, and guarantees you the love, of God must be the *false promise of the devil.* God would never make such a promise, you tell yourself, only the devil would—to tempt you into denying God's true identity as the fearsome, judgmental, jealous, vengeful, and punishing entity of entities.

Even though this description better fits the definition of a devil (if there *were* one), you have assigned *devilish characteristics* to God in order to convince yourself not to accept the God-like promises of your Creator, or the God-like qualities of the Self.

Such is the power of fear.

I am trying to let go of my fear. Will You tell me—again—more of the laws?

The First Law is that you can be, do, and have whatever you can imagine. The Second Law is that you attract what you fear.

Why is that?

Emotion is the power which attracts. That which you fear strongly, you will experience. An animal—which you consider a lower form of life (even though animals act with more integrity and greater consistency than humans)—knows immediately if you are afraid of it. Plants—which you consider an even *lower* form of life—respond to people who love them far better than to those who couldn't care less.

None of this is by coincidence. There *is* no coincidence in the universe—only a grand design; an incredible "snowflake."

Emotion is energy in motion. When you move energy, you create effect. If you move enough energy, you create matter. Matter is energy conglomerated. Moved around. Shoved together. If you manipulate energy long enough in a certain way, you get matter. Every Master understands this law. It is the alchemy of the universe. It is the secret of all life.

Thought is pure energy. Every thought you have, have ever had, and ever will have is creative. The energy of your thought never ever dies. Ever. It leaves your being and heads out into the universe, extending forever. A thought is forever.

All thoughts congeal; all thoughts meet other thoughts, criss-crossing in an incredible maze of energy, forming an ever-changing pattern of unspeakable beauty and unbelievable complexity.

Like energy attracts like energy—forming (to use simple words) "clumps" of energy of like kind. When enough similar "clumps" criss-cross each other—run into each other—they *"stick to"* each other (to use another simple term). It takes an incomprehensibly huge amount of similar energy "sticking together," thusly, to form matter. But matter _will_ form out of pure energy. In fact, that is the only way it _can_ form. Once energy becomes matter, it remains matter for a very long time—unless its construction is _disrupted_ by an opposing, or dissimilar, form of energy. This dissimilar energy, acting upon matter, actually dismembers the matter, releasing the raw energy of which it was composed.

This is, in elementary terms, the theory behind your atomic bomb. Einstein came closer than any other human—before or since—to discovering, explaining, and functionalizing the creative secret of the universe.

You should now better understand how people of _like mind_ can work together to create a favored reality. The phrase "Wherever two or more are gathered in My name" becomes much more meaningful.

Of course, when entire _societies_ think a certain way, very often astonishing things happen—not all of them necessarily desirable. For instance, a society living in fear, very often—actually, _inevitably_—produces in form that which it fears most.

Similarly, large communities or congregations often find miracle-producing power in combined thinking (or what some people call common prayer).

And it must be made clear that even individuals—if their thought (prayer, hope, wish, dream, fear) is amazingly strong—can, in and of themselves, produce such results. Jesus did this regularly. He understood how to manipulate energy and matter, how to rearrange it, how to redistribute it, how to utterly control it. Many Masters have known this. Many know it now.

You can know it. Right now.

This is the knowledge of good and evil of which Adam and Eve partook. Until they understood this, there could be no life _as you know it_. Adam and Eve—the mythical names you have given to represent First Man and First Woman—were the Father and Mother of the human experience.

What has been described as the fall of Adam was actually his upliftment—the greatest single event in the history of humankind. For without it, the world of relativity would not exist. The act of Adam and Eve was not original sin, but, in truth, first blessing. You should thank them from the bottom of your hearts—for in being the first to make a "wrong" choice, Adam and Eve *produced the possibility* of making *any choice at all*.

In your mythology you have made Eve the "bad" one here—the temptress who ate of the fruit, the knowledge of good and evil—and coyly invited Adam to join her. This mythological set-up has allowed you to make woman man's "downfall" ever since, resulting in all manner of warped realities—not to mention distorted sexual views and confusions. (How can you feel so *good* about something so *bad*?)

What you most fear is what will most plague you. Fear will draw it *to* you like a magnet. All your holy scriptures—of every religious persuasion and tradition which you have created—contain the clear admonition: fear not. Do you think this is by accident?

The Laws are very simple.

    1. Thought is creative.
    2. Fear attracts like energy.
    3. Love is all there is.

Oops, you got me on that third one. How can love be all there is if fear attracts like energy?

Love is the ultimate reality. It is the only. The all. The feeling of love is your experience of God.

In highest Truth, love is all there is, all there was, and all there ever will be. When you move into the absolute, you move into love.

The realm of the relative was created in order that I might experience My Self. This has already been explained to you. This does not make the realm of the relative *real*. It is a *created reality* you and I have devised and continue to devise—in order that we may know ourselves experientially.

Yet the creation can seem very real. Its *purpose* is to seem so real, we *accept* it as truly existing. In this way, God has contrived to create "something else" other than Itself (though in strictest terms this is impossible, since God is—I AM—All That Is).

In creating "something else"—namely, the realm of the relative—I have produced an environment in which you may *choose* to be God, rather than simply be *told* that you are God; in which you may experience God-head as an act of creation, rather than a conceptualization; in which the little candle in the sun—the littlest soul—can know itself as the light.

Fear is the *other end* of love. It is the *primal polarity.* In creating the realm of the relative, I first created the opposite of My Self. Now, in the realm in which you live on the physical plane, there are only *two places of being:* fear and love. Thoughts rooted in fear will produce one kind of manifestation on the physical plane. Thoughts rooted in love will produce another.

The Masters who have walked the planet are those who have discovered the secret of the relative world—and refused to acknowledge its reality. In short, *Masters are those who have chosen only love. In every instance. In every moment. In every circumstance.* Even as they were being killed, they loved their murderers. Even as they were being persecuted, they loved their oppressors.

This is very difficult for you to understand, much less emulate. Nevertheless, it is what *every Master has ever done.* It doesn't matter what the philosophy, it doesn't matter what the tradition, it doesn't matter what the religion—it is what *every Master has done.*

This example and this lesson has been laid out so clearly for you. Time and time again, over and over has it been shown to you. Through all the ages and in every place. Through all your lifetimes and in every moment. The universe has used every contrivance to place this Truth before you. In song and story, in poetry and dance, in words and in motion—in pictures of motion, which you call motion pictures, and in collections of words, which you call books.

From the highest mountain it has been shouted, in the lowest place its whisper has been heard. *Through the corridors of all human experience has this Truth been echoed:* Love is the answer. *Yet you have not listened.*

Now come you to this book, asking God again what God has told you countless times in countless ways. Yet I will tell you again—*here*—in the context of *this* book. Will you listen now? Will you truly hear?

What do you think brought you to this material? How does it come to pass that you are holding it in your hands? Do you think I know not what I am doing?

There are no coincidences in the universe.

I have heard the crying of your heart. I have seen the searching of your soul. I *know* how deeply you have desired the Truth. In pain have you called out for it, and in joy. Unendingly have you beseeched Me. *Show* Myself. *Explain* Myself. Reveal Myself.

I am doing so here, in terms so plain, you cannot misunderstand. In language so simple, you cannot be confused. In vocabulary so common, you cannot get lost in the verbiage.

So go ahead now. Ask Me anything. *Anything.* I will contrive to bring you the answer. The whole universe will I use to do this. So be on the lookout. This book is far from My only tool. You may ask a question, then *put this book down.* But watch. Listen. The words to the next song you hear. The information in the next article you read. The story line of the next movie you watch. The chance utterance of the next person you meet. Or the whisper of the next river, the next ocean, the next breeze that caresses your ear—*all these devices* are Mine; all these avenues are open to Me. I will speak to you if you will listen. I will come to you if you will invite Me. I will show you then that I have *always* been there. *All ways.*

2

"Thou wilt show me the path of life:
in thy presence is fullness of joy;
at thy right hand there are
pleasures forevermore."
—Psalm 16:11

I've searched for the path to God all my life—

I know you have—

—and now I've found it and I can't believe it. It feels like I'm sitting here, writing this to myself.

You are.

That does not seem like what a communication with God would feel like.

You want bells and whistles? I'll see what I can arrange.

You know, don't You, that there are those who will call this entire book a blasphemy. Especially if You keep showing up as such a wise guy.

Let Me explain something to you. You have this idea that God shows up in only one way in life. That's a very dangerous idea.

It stops you from seeing God all over. If you think God looks only one way or sounds only one way or *is* only one way, you're going to look right past Me night and day. You'll spend your whole life looking for God and not finding Her. Because you're looking for a *Him*. I use this as an example.

It has been said that if you don't see God in the profane and the profound, you're missing half the story. That is a great Truth.

God is in the sadness and the laughter, in the bitter and the sweet. There is a divine purpose behind everything—and therefore a divine presence *in* everything.

I once began writing a book called *God is a Salami Sandwich.*

That would have been a very good book. I *gave* you that inspiration. Why did you not write it?

It felt like blasphemy. Or at the very least, horribly irreverent.

You mean *wonderfully* irreverent! What gave you the idea that God is only "reverent"? God is the up *and* the down. The hot *and* the cold. The left *and* the right. The reverent *and* the irreverent!

Think you that God cannot laugh? Do you imagine that God does not enjoy a good joke? Is it your knowing that God is without humor? I tell you, God *invented* humor.

Must you speak in hushed tones when you speak to Me? Are slang words or tough language outside My ken? I tell you, you can speak to Me as you would speak with your best friend.

Do you think there is a word I have not heard? A sight I have not seen? A sound I do not know?

Is it your thought that I despise some of these, while I love the others? *I tell you, I despise nothing. None of it is repulsive to Me.* It is *life*, and *life is the gift*; the unspeakable treasure; the holy of holies.

I am life, for I am the stuff life *is*. Its every aspect has a divine purpose. Nothing exists—*nothing*—without a reason understood and approved by God.

How can this be? What of the evil which has been created by man?

You cannot create a *thing*—not a thought, an object, an event—no experience of *any kind*—which is outside of God's plan. For God's plan is for you to create *anything—everything—whatever you want*. In such freedom lies the experience of God being God—and this is the experience *for which I created You*. And life itself.

Evil is that which you *call* evil. Yet even that I love, for it is only through that which you call evil that you can know good; only through that which you call the work of the devil that you can know and do the work of God. I do not love hot more than I love cold, high more than low, left more than right. It is *all relative*. It is all part of *what is*.

I do not love "good" more than I love "bad." *Hitler went to heaven*. When you understand this, you will understand God.

But I have been raised to believe that good and bad *do* exist; that right and wrong *are* opposed; that some things are not okay, not alright, not acceptable in the sight of God.

Everything is "acceptable" in the sight of God, for how can God not accept that which is? To reject a thing is to deny that it exists. To say that it is not okay is to say that it is not a part of Me—and that is impossible.

Yet hold to your beliefs, and stay true to your values, for these are the values of your parents, of your parents' parents; of your friends and of your society. They form the structure of your life, and to lose them would be to unravel the fabric of your experience. Still, examine them one by one. Review them piece by piece. Do not

61

dismantle the house, but look at each brick, and replace those which appear broken, which no longer support the structure.

Your ideas about right and wrong are just that—ideas. They are the thoughts which form the shape and create the substance of Who You Are. There would be only one reason to change any of these; only one purpose in making an alteration: if you are not happy with Who You Are.

Only you can know if you are happy. Only you can say of your life—"This is my creation (son), in which I am well pleased."

If your values serve you, hold to them. Argue for them. Fight to defend them.

Yet seek to fight in a way which harms no one. Harm is not a necessary ingredient in healing.

You say "hold to your values" at the same time you say our values are all wrong. Help me with this.

I have not said your values are wrong. But neither are they right. They are simply judgments. Assessments. Decisions. For the most part, they are decisions made not by you, but by someone else. Your parents, perhaps. Your religion. Your teachers, historians, politicians.

Very few of the value judgments you have incorporated into your truth are judgments you, yourself, have made based on your own experience. Yet experience is what you came here for—and out of your experience were you to create yourself. *You* have created yourself out of the experience of *others.*

If there were such a thing as sin, this would be it: to allow yourself to become what you are because of the experience of others. This is the "sin" you have committed. All of you. You do not await your own experience, you accept the experience of *others* as gospel (literally), and then, when you encounter the *actual experience* for the first time, you overlay what you think you *already know* onto the encounter.

If you did not do this, you might have a wholly different experience—one that might render your original teacher or source *wrong*. In most cases, you don't want to make your parents, your schools, your religions, your traditions, your holy scriptures wrong—so you *deny your own experience* in favor of what you have been *told to think*.

Nowhere can this be more profoundly illustrated than in your treatment of human sexuality.

Everyone knows that the sexual experience can be the single most loving, most exciting, most powerful, most exhilarating, most renewing, most energizing, most affirming, most intimate, most uniting, most re-creative *physical* experience of which humans are capable. Having discovered this experientially, you have chosen to accept instead the prior judgments, opinions, and ideas about sex promulgated by *others*—all of whom have a vested interest in how you think.

These opinions, judgments, and ideas have run directly contradictory to your own experience, yet because you are *loathe to make your teachers wrong,* you convince yourself it must be your *experience* that is wrong. The result is that you have betrayed your true truth about this subject—with devastating results.

You have done the same thing with money. Every time in your life that you have had lots and lots of money, you have felt great. You felt great receiving it, and you felt great spending it. There was nothing bad about it, nothing evil, nothing inherently "wrong." Yet you have so deeply ingrained within you the teachings of *others* on this subject that you have *rejected* your experience in favor of "truth."

Having adopted this "truth" as your own, you have formed thoughts around it—thoughts which are *creative*. You have thus created a personal reality around money which pushes it away from you—for why would you seek to attract that which is not good?

Amazingly, you have created this same contradiction

around God. Everything your heart experiences about God tells you that God is good. Everything your teachers teach you about God tells you God is bad. Your heart tells you God is to be loved without fear. Your teachers tell you God is to be feared, for He is a vengeful God. You are to live in fear of God's wrath, they say. You are to tremble in His presence. Your whole life through you are to fear the judgment of the Lord. For the Lord is "just," you are told. And God knows, you will be in trouble when you confront the terrible justice of the Lord. You are, therefore, to be "obedient" to God's commands. Or else.

Above all, you are not to ask such logical questions as, "if God wanted strict obedience to His Laws, why did He create the possibility of those Laws being violated?" Ah, your teachers tell you—because God wanted you to have "free choice." Yet what kind of choice is free when to choose one thing over the other brings condemnation? How is "free will" free when it is not your will, but someone else's, which must be done? Those who teach you this would make a hypocrite of God.

You are told that God is forgiveness, and compassion—yet if you do not ask for this forgiveness in the "right way," if you do not "come to God" *properly*, your plea will not be heard, your cry will go unheeded. Even this would not be so bad if there were only one proper way, but there are as many "proper ways" being taught as there are teachers to teach them.

Most of you, therefore, spend the bulk of your adult life searching for the "right" way to worship, to obey, and to serve God. *The irony of all this is that I do not want your worship, I do not need your obedience, and it is not necessary for you to serve Me.*

These behaviors are the behaviors historically demanded of their subjects by monarchs—usually egomaniacal, insecure, tyrannical monarchs at that. They're not Godly demands in any sense—and it seems remarkable that the world hasn't by now concluded that the demands are counterfeit, having nothing to do with the needs or desires of Deity.

Deity has no needs. All That Is is exactly that: all that is. It therefore wants, or lacks, nothing—by definition.

If you choose to believe in a God who somehow *needs* something—and has such hurt feelings if He doesn't get it that He punishes those from whom He expected to receive it—then you choose to believe in a God much smaller than I. You truly *are* Children of a Lesser God.

No, my children, please let Me assure you again, through this writing, that I am without needs. I require nothing.

This does not mean I am without *desires. Desires* and *needs* are not the same thing (although many of you have made them so in your present lifetime).

Desire is the beginning of all creation. It is first thought. It is a grand feeling within the soul. It is God, choosing what next to create.

And what is God's desire?

I desire first to know and experience Myself, in all My glory—to know Who I Am. Before I invented you—and all the worlds of the universe—it was impossible for Me to do so.

Second, I desire that you shall know and experience Who You Really Are, through the power I have given you to create and experience yourself in whatever way you choose.

Third, I desire for the whole life process to be an experience of constant joy, continuous creation, neverending expansion, and total fulfillment in each moment of now.

I have established a perfect system whereby these desires may be realized. They are being realized now—in this very moment. The only difference between you and Me is that *I know this.*

In the moment of your total knowing (which moment could come upon you at anytime), you, too, will feel as I do always: totally joyful, loving, accepting, blessing, and grateful.

These are the *Five Attitudes* of God, and before we are through with this dialogue, I will show you how the application of these attitudes in your life now can—and *will*—bring you to Godliness.

All of this is a very long answer to a very short question.

Yes, hold to your values—so long as you experience that they serve you. Yet look to see whether the values *you* serve, with your thoughts, words, and actions, bring to the space of your experience the highest and best idea you ever had about you.

Examine your values one by one. Hold them up to the light of public scrutiny. If you can tell the world who you are and what you believe without breaking stride or hesitating, you are happy with yourself. There is no reason to continue much further in this dialogue with Me, because you have created a Self—and a life *for* the Self—which needs no improvement. You have reached perfection. Put the book down.

My life is not perfect, nor is it close to being perfect. I am not perfect. I am, in fact, a bundle of imperfections. I wish—sometimes I wish with all my heart—that I could correct these imperfections; that I knew what causes my behaviors, what sets up my downfalls, what keeps getting in my way. That's why I've come to You, I guess. I haven't been able to find the answers on my own.

I am glad you came. I have always been here to help you. I am here now. You don't have to find the answers on your own. You never had to.

Yet it seems so. . .*presumptuous*. . .to simply sit down and dialogue with You this way—much less to imagine that You—*God*—are responding—I mean, this is *crazy*.

I see. The authors of the Bible were all sane, but *you* are crazy.

The Bible writers were witnesses to the life of Christ, and faithfully recorded what they heard and saw.

Correction. Most of the New Testament writers never met or saw Jesus in their lives. They lived many years after Jesus left the Earth. They wouldn't have known Jesus of Nazareth if they walked into him on the street.

But. . .

The Bible writers were great believers and great historians. They took the stories which had been passed down to them and to their friends by others—elders—from elder to elder, until finally a written record was made.

And not everything of the Bible authors was included in the final document.

Already "churches" had sprung up around the teachings of Jesus—and, as happens whenever and wherever people gather in groups around a powerful idea, there were certain individuals within these churches, or enclaves, who determined what parts of the Jesus Story were going to be told—and how. This process of selecting and editing continued throughout the gathering, writing, and publishing of the gospels, and the Bible.

Even several *centuries* after the original scriptures were committed to writing, a High Council of the Church determined yet one more time which doctrines and truths were to be included in the then-official Bible—and which would be "unhealthy" or "premature" to reveal to the masses.

And there have been other holy scriptures as well—each placed in writing in moments of inspiration by otherwise ordinary men, none of whom were any more crazy than you.

Are you suggesting—you're not suggesting, are you—that *these* writings might one day become "holy scriptures"?

My child, *everything in life is holy.* By that measure, yes, these are holy writings. But I will not quibble with you over words, because I know what you mean.

No, I do not suggest that this manuscript will one day become holy scripture. At least, not for several hundred years, or until the language becomes outmoded.

You see, the problem is that the language here is too colloquial, too conversational, too contemporary. People assume that if God were to talk directly with you, God would not sound like the fella next door. There should be some unifying, if not to say deifying, structure to the language. Some dignity. Some sense of Godliness.

As I said earlier, that's part of the problem. People have a sense of God as "showing up" in only one form. Anything which violates that form is seen as blasphemy.

As I said earlier.

As you said earlier.

But let's drive to the heart of your question. Why do you think it's crazy for you to be able to have a dialogue with God? Do you not believe in prayer?

Yes, but that's different. Prayer for me has always been one-way. I ask, and God remains immutable.

God has never answered a prayer?

Oh yes, but never *verbally*, you see. Oh, I've had all *kinds* of things happen in my life that I was convinced were an answer—a very direct answer—to prayer. But God has never *spoken* to me.

I see. So this God in which you believe—this God can *do* anything—It just cannot speak.

Of *course* God can speak, if God wants to. It just doesn't seem probable that God would want to speak to *me*.

This is the root of every problem you experience in your life—for you do not consider yourself worthy enough to be spoken to by God.
Good heavens, how can you ever expect to hear My voice if you don't imagine yourself to be deserving enough to even be *spoken to*?
I tell you this: I am performing a miracle right now. For not only am I speaking to you, but to every person who has picked up this book and is reading these words.
To each of them am I now speaking. I know who every one of them is. I know now who will find their way to these words—and I know that (just as with all My other communications) some will be able to hear—and some will be able to only listen, but will *hear nothing*.

Well, that brings up another thing. I am already thinking of publishing this material even now, as it's being written.

Yes. What's "wrong" with that?

Can't it be argued that I am creating this whole thing for profit? Doesn't that render the whole thing suspect?

Is it your motive to write something so that you can make a lot of money?

No. That's not why I started this. I began this dialogue on paper because my mind has been plagued with questions for 30 years—questions I've been hungry—*starving* to have answered. The idea that I would have all this made into a book came later.

From Me.

From You?

Yes. You don't think I was going to let you waste all these marvelous questions and answers, do you?

I hadn't thought about that. At the outset, I just wanted the questions answered; the frustration to end; the search to be over.

Good. So stop questioning your motives (you do it incessantly) and let's get *on* with it.

3

Well, I have a hundred questions. A thousand. A *million*. And the problem is, I sometimes don't know where to begin.

> Just list the questions. Just start *somewhere*. Go ahead, right now. Make a list of the questions that occur to you.

Okay. Some of them are going to seem pretty simple, pretty plebeian.

> Stop making judgments against yourself. Just list them.

Right. Well, here are the ones that occur to me now.

1. When will my life finally take off? What does it take to "get it together," and achieve even a modicum of success? Can the struggle ever end?

2. When will I learn enough about relationships to be able to have them go smoothly? Is there any way *to* be happy in relationships? Must they always be constantly challenging?

3. Why can't I ever seem to attract enough money in my life? Am I destined to be scrimping and scraping for the rest of my life? What is blocking me from realizing my full potential in this regard?

4. Why can't I do what I really *want* to do with my life and still make a living?

5. How can I solve some of the health problems I face? I have been the victim of enough chronic problems to last a lifetime. Why am I having them all now?

6. What is the karmic lesson I'm supposed to be learning here? What am I trying to master?

7. Is there such a thing as reincarnation? How many past lives have I had? What was I in them? Is "karmic debt" a reality?

8. I sometimes feel very psychic. Is there such a thing as "being psychic"? Am I that? Are people who claim to be psychic "trafficking with the devil"?

9. Is it okay to take money for doing good? If I choose to do healing work in the world—God's work—can I do that and become financially abundant, too? Or are the two mutually exclusive?

10. Is sex okay? C'mon—what is the real story behind this human experience? Is sex purely for procreation, as some religions say? Is true holiness and enlightenment achieved through denial—or transmutation—of the sexual energy? Is it okay to have sex without love? Is just the physical sensation of it okay enough as a reason?

11. Why did you make sex so good, so spectacular, so powerful a human experience if all we are to do is stay away from it as much as we can? What gives? For that matter, why are all fun things either "immoral, illegal, or fattening"?

12. Is there life on other planets? Have we been visited by it? Are we being observed now? Will we see evidence—irrevocable and indisputable—of extraterrestrial life in our lifetime? Does each form of life have its own God? Are you the God of It All?

13. Will utopia ever come to the planet Earth? Will God ever show Himself to Earth's people, as promised? Is there such a thing as the Second Coming? Will there ever be an End of the World—or an apocalypse, as prophesied in the Bible? Is there a one true religion? If so, which one?

These are just a few of my questions. As I said, I have a hundred more. Some of these questions embarrass me—they seem so sophomoric. But answer them, please—one at a time—and let's "talk" about them.

> Good. Now we're getting to it. Don't apologize for
> these questions. These are the questions men and
> women have been asking for hundreds of years. If the
> questions were so silly, they wouldn't be asked over and

over again by each succeeding generation. So let's go to question one.

I have established Laws in the universe that make it possible for you to have—to create—exactly what you choose. These Laws cannot be violated, nor can they be ignored. You are following these Laws right now, even as you read this. You cannot not follow the Law, for these are the ways things work. You cannot step aside from this; you cannot operate outside of it.

Every minute of your life you have been operating *inside* of it—and everything you have ever experienced you have thusly created.

You are in a partnership with God. We share an eternal covenant. My promise to you is to always give you what you ask. Your promise is to ask; to understand the process of the asking and the answering. I've already explained this process to you once. I'll do so again, so that you clearly understand it.

You are a three-fold being. You consist of *body, mind,* and *spirit.* You could also call these the *physical,* the *non-physical,* and the *meta-physical. This is the Holy Trinity, and it has been called by many names.*

That which you are, I am. I am manifested as Three-In-One. Some of your theologians have called this Father, Son, and Holy Spirit.

Your psychiatrists have recognized this triumvirate and called it conscious, subconscious, and superconscious.

Your philosophers have called it the id, the ego, and the super ego.

Science ,calls this energy, matter, and antimatter.

Poets speak of mind, heart, and soul. New Age thinkers refer to body, mind, and spirit.

Your time is divided into past, present, and future. Could this not be the same as subconscious, conscious, and superconscious?

Space is likewise divided into three: here, there, and the space between.

It is defining and describing this "space between"

that becomes difficult, elusive. The moment you begin defining or describing, the space you describe becomes "here" or "there." Yet we *know* this "space between" exists. It is what holds "here" and "there" in place—just as the eternal now holds "before" and "after" in place.

These three aspects of you are actually three energies. You might call them *thought, word,* and *action.* All three put together produce a *result*—which in your language and understanding is called a feeling, or experience.

Your soul (subconscious, id, spirit, past, etc.) *is the sum total of every feeling you've ever had* (created). Your awareness of some of these is called your memory. When you have a memory, you are said to re-member. That is, to put back together. To reassemble the parts.

When you reassemble all of the parts of you, you will have re-membered Who You Really Are.

The process of creation starts with thought—an idea, conception, visualization. Everything you see was once someone's idea. Nothing exists in your world that did not first exist as pure thought.

This is true of the universe as well.

Thought is the first level of creation.

Next comes the *word.* Everything you say is a thought expressed. It is creative and sends forth creative energy into the universe. Words are more dynamic (thus, some might say more creative) than thought, because words are a different level of vibration from thought. They disrupt (change, alter, affect) the universe with greater impact.

Words are the second level of creation.

Next comes *action.*

Actions are words moving. Words are thoughts expressed. Thoughts are ideas formed. Ideas are energies come together. Energies are forces released. Forces are elements existent. Elements are particles of God, portions of All, the stuff of everything.

The beginning is God. The end is action. Action is God creating—or God experienced.

Your thought about yourself is that you are not good enough, not wondrous enough, not sinless enough, to be a part of God, in partnership with God. You have denied for so long Who You Are that you have *forgotten* Who You Are.

This has not occurred by coincidence; this is not happenstance. It is all part of the divine plan—for you could not claim, create, experience—Who You Are if you already were it. It was necessary first for you to release (deny, forget) your connection to Me in order to fully experience it by fully creating it—by calling it forth. For your grandest wish—and My grandest desire—was for you to experience yourself as the part of Me you are. You are therefore in the process of experiencing yourself by creating yourself anew in every single moment. As am I. Through you.

Do you see the partnership? Do you grasp its implications? It is a holy collaboration—truly, a holy communion.

Life will "take off" for you, then, when you choose for it to. You have not so chosen as yet. You have procrastinated, prolonged, protracted, protested. Now it is time that you promulgated and produced what you have been promised. To do this, you must believe the promise, and live it. *You must live the promise of God.*

The promise of God is that you are His son. Her offspring. Its likeness. His equal.

Ah. . .here is where you get hung up. You can accept "His son," "offspring," "likeness," but you recoil at being called "His equal." It is too much to accept. Too much bigness, too much wonderment—too much *responsibility*. For if you are God's *equal*, that means nothing is being done *to* you—and all things are created *by* you. *There can be no more victims and no more villains*—only outcomes of your thought about a thing.

I tell you this: all *you see in your world is the outcome of your idea about it.*

Do you want your life to truly "take off"? Then

change your idea about it. About you. Think, speak, and act as the _God You Are_.

Of course this will separate you from many—most—of your fellow men. They will call you crazy. They will say you blaspheme. They will eventually have enough of you, and they will attempt to crucify you.

They will do this not because they think you are living in a world of your own illusions (most men are gracious enough to allow you your private entertainments), but because, sooner or later, others will become _attracted_ to your truth—for the promises it holds for _them_.

Here is where your fellow men will interfere—for here is where you will begin to threaten them. For your simple truth, simply lived, will offer more beauty, more comfort, more peace, more joy, and more love of self and others than anything your earthly fellows could contrive.

And that truth, adopted, would mean the end of their ways. It would mean the end of hatred and fear and bigotry and war. The end of the condemning and killing that has gone on in _My name_. The end of might-is-right. The end of purchase-through-power. The end of loyalty and homage through fear. The end of the world as they know it—and as _you_ have created it thus far.

So be ready, kind soul. For you will be vilified and spat upon, called names, and deserted, and finally they will accuse you, try you, and condemn you—all in their own ways—from the moment you accept and adopt your holy cause—the realization of Self.

Why, then, do it?

Because you are no longer concerned with the acceptance or approval of the world. You are no longer satisfied with what that has brought you. You are no longer pleased with what it has given others. You want the pain to stop, the suffering to stop, the illusion to end. You have had enough of this world as it presently is. You seek a newer world.

Seek it *no longer*. Now, *call it forth*.

Can you help me to better understand how to do that?

Yes. Go first to your Highest Thought about yourself. Imagine the you that you would be if you lived that thought every day. Imagine what you would think, do, and say, and how you would respond to what others do and say.

Do you see any difference between that projection and what you think, do, and say now?

Yes. I see a great deal of difference.

Good. You should, since we know that right now you are not living your highest vision of yourself. Now, having seen the differences between where you are and where you want to be, begin to change—consciously change—your thoughts, words, and actions to match your grandest vision.

This will require tremendous mental and physical effort. It will entail constant, moment-to-moment monitoring of your every thought, word, and deed. It will involve continued choice-making—consciously. This whole process is a massive move to consciousness. What you will find out if you undertake this challenge is that *you've spent half your life unconscious*. That is to say, unaware on a conscious level of *what you are choosing* in the way of thoughts, words, and deeds until you experience the aftermath of them. Then, when you experience these results, you deny that your thoughts, words, and deeds had anything to do with them.

This is a call to stop such unconscious living. It is a challenge to which your soul has called you from the beginning of time.

That kind of continual mental monitoring seems as though it might be terribly exhausting—

It could be, until it becomes second nature. In fact, it _is_ your second nature. It is your first nature to be unconditionally loving. It is your second nature to choose to express your first nature, your true nature, consciously.

Excuse me, but wouldn't this kind of non-stop editing of everything I think, say, and do "make Jack a dull boy"?

Never. Different, yes. Dull, no. Was Jesus dull? I don't think so. Was the Buddha boring to be around? People flocked, begged, to be in his presence. No one who has attained mastery is dull. Unusual, perhaps. Extraordinary, perhaps. But never dull.

So—do you want your life to "take off"? _Begin at once to imagine it the way you want it to be—and move into that. Check every thought, word, and action that does not fall into harmony with that. Move away from those._

When you have a thought that is not in alignment with your higher vision, _change to a new thought_, then and there. When you say a thing that is out of alignment with your grandest idea, make a note not to say something like that again. When you do a thing that is misaligned with your best intention, decide to make that the last time. And make it right with whomever was involved if you can.

I've heard this before and I've always railed against it, because it seems so dishonest. I mean, if you're sick as a dog, you're not supposed to admit it. If you're broke as a pauper, you're never supposed to say it. If you're upset as hell, you're not supposed to show it. It reminds me of the joke about the three people who were sent to hell. One was a Catholic, one was a Jew, one was a New Ager. The devil said to the Catholic, sneeringly, "Well, how are you enjoying the heat?" And the Catholic sniffled, "I'm offering it up." The devil then asked the Jew, "And how are _you_ enjoying the heat?" The Jew said, "So what else could I expect but more hell?" Finally, the devil approached the New Ager. "Heat?" the New Ager asked, perspiring. "What heat?"

That's a good joke. But I'm not talking about ignoring the problem, or pretending it isn't there. I'm talking about noticing the circumstance, and then telling your highest truth about it.

If you're broke, you're broke. It's pointless to lie about it, and actually debilitating to try to manufacture a story about it so as not to admit it. Yet it's your thought about it—"Broke is bad," "This is horrible," "I'm a bad person, because good people who work hard and really try _never_ go broke," etc.—that rules how you _experience_ "broke-ness." It's your words about it—"I'm broke," "I haven't a dime," "I don't have any money"—that dictates how long you _stay_ broke. It's your actions surrounding it—feeling sorry for yourself, sitting around despondent, not trying to find a way out because "What's the use, anyway?"—that create your long-term reality.

The first thing to understand about the universe is that no condition is "good" or "bad." It just _is_. So stop making value judgments.

The second thing to know is that _all conditions are temporary. Nothing stays the same, nothing remains static. Which_ way _a thing changes depends on_ you.

Excuse me, but I have to interrupt you again here. What about the person who is sick, but has the faith that will move mountains—and so thinks, says, and _believes_ he's going to get better. . .only to die six weeks later. How does _that_ square with all this positive thinking, affirmative action stuff?

That's good. You're asking the tough questions. That's good. You're not simply taking My word for any of this. There is a place, on down the line, when you'll _have_ to take My word for this—because eventually you'll find that we can discuss this thing forever, you and I—until there's nothing left to do but to "try it or deny it." But we're not at that place yet. So let's keep the dialogue going; let's keep talking—

The person who has the "faith to move mountains," and dies six weeks later, has moved mountains for six weeks. That may have been enough for him. He may have decided, on the last hour of the last day, "Okay, I've had enough. I'm ready to go on now to another adventure." You may not have known of that decision, because he may not have told you. The truth is, he may have made that decision quite a bit earlier—days, weeks earlier—and not have told you; not have told anyone.

You have created a society in which it is very not okay to want to die—very not okay to be very okay with death. Because you don't want to die, you can't imagine *anyone* wanting to die—no matter what their circumstances or condition.

But there are many situations in which death is preferable to life—which I know you can imagine if you think about it for even a little bit. Yet, these truths don't occur to you—they are not that self-evident—when you are looking in the face someone else who is choosing to die. And the dying person knows this. She can feel the level of acceptance in the room regarding her decision.

Have you ever noticed how many people wait until the room is empty before they die? Some even have to tell their loved ones—"No, really, go. Get a bite to eat." Or "Go, get some sleep. I'm fine. I'll see you in the morning." And then, when the loyal guard leaves, so does the soul from the body of the guarded.

If they told their assembled relatives and friends, "I just want to die," they would really hear it. "Oh, you don't mean that," or "Now, don't talk that way," or "Hang in there," or "Please don't leave me."

The entire medical profession is trained to keep people alive, rather than keeping people comfortable so that they can die with dignity.

You see, to a doctor or a nurse, death is failure. To a friend or relative, death is disaster. Only to the soul is death a relief—a release.

The greatest gift you can give the dying is to let them die in peace—not thinking that they must "hang on," or continue to suffer, or worry about *you* at this most crucial passage in their life.

So this is very often what has happened in the case of the man who says he's going to live, believes he's going to live, even prays to live: that at the soul level, he has "changed his mind." It is time now to drop the body to free the soul for other pursuits. When the soul makes this decision, nothing the body does can change it. Nothing the mind thinks can alter it. It is at the moment of death that we learn who, in the body-mind-soul triumvirate, is running things.

All your life you think you are your body. Some of the time you think you are your mind. It is at the time of your death that you find out Who You Really Are.

Now there are also times when the body and the mind are just not *listening* to the soul. This, too, creates the scenario you describe. The most difficult thing for people to do is hear their own soul. (Notice that so few do.)

Now it happens often that the soul makes a decision that it is time to leave the body. The body and the mind—ever servants of the soul—hear this, and the process of extrication begins. Yet the mind (ego) doesn't want to accept. After all, this is the end of its existence. So it instructs the body to resist death. This the body does gladly, since it too does not want to die. The body and the mind (ego) receive great encouragement, great praise for this from the outside world—the world of its creation. So the strategy is confirmed.

Now at this point everything depends on how badly the soul wants to leave. If there is no great urgency here, the soul may say, "Alright, you win. I'll stick around with you a little longer." But if the soul is very clear that staying does not serve its higher agenda—that there is no further way it can *evolve* through this body—the soul is going to leave, and nothing will stop it—nor should anything try to.

The soul is very clear that its purpose is evolution. That is its *sole* purpose—and its *soul* purpose. It is not concerned with the achievements of the body or the development of the mind. These are all meaningless to the soul.

The soul is also clear that there is no great tragedy involved in leaving the body. In many ways, the tragedy is being *in* the body. So you have to understand, the soul sees this whole death thing differently. It, of course, sees the whole "life thing" differently, too—and that is the source of much of the frustration and anxiety one feels in one's life. The frustration and anxiety comes from not listening to one's soul.

How can I best listen to my soul? If the soul is the boss, really, how can I make sure I get those memos from the front office?

The first thing you might do is get clear about what the soul is after—and stop making judgments about it.

I'm making judgments about my own soul?

Constantly. I just showed you how you judge yourself for wanting to die. You also judge yourself for wanting to live—truly *live*. You judge yourself for wanting to laugh, wanting to cry, wanting to win, wanting to lose—for wanting to experience joy and love—*especially* do you judge yourself for that.

I do?

Somewhere you've come across the idea that to *deny* yourself joy is Godly—that *not* to celebrate life is heavenly. Denial, you have told yourself, is goodness.

Are you saying it is bad?

It is neither good nor bad, it is simply denial. If you feel good after denying yourself, then in your world that is goodness. If you feel bad, then it's badness. Most of the time, you can't decide. You deny yourself this or that because you tell yourself you are supposed to. Then you say that was a good thing to do—but wonder why you don't *feel* good.

And so the first thing to do is to stop making these judgments against yourself. Learn what is the soul's desire, and go with that. Go with the soul.

What the soul is after is—the highest feeling of love you can imagine. This is the soul's desire. This is its purpose. The soul is after the feeling. Not the knowledge, but the feeling. It already has the knowledge, but knowledge is conceptual. Feeling is experiential. The soul wants to feel itself, and thus to know itself *in its own experience.*

The highest feeling is the experience of unity with All That Is. This is the great return to Truth for which the soul yearns. This is the feeling of perfect love.

Perfect love is to feeling what perfect white is to color. Many think that white is the *absence* of color. It is not. It is the inclusion of all color. White is *every other color that exists,* combined.

So, too, is love not the absence of an emotion (hatred, anger, lust, jealousy, covetousness), but the summation of all feeling. It is the sum total. The aggregate amount. The everything.

Thus, for the soul to experience perfect love, it must experience *every human feeling.*

How can I have compassion on that which I don't understand? How can I forgive in another that which I have never experienced in Myself? So we see both the simplicity and the awesome magnitude of the soul's journey. We understand at last what it is up to:

The purpose of the human soul is to experience all of it—so that it can be *all of it.*

How can it be up if it has never been down, left
if it has never been right? How can it be warm if it
knows not cold, good if it denies evil? Obviously the
soul cannot choose to be anything _if there is nothing
to choose from._ For the soul to experience its grandeur, it must _know what grandeur is._ This it cannot
do if there is nothing _but_ grandeur. And so the soul
realizes that grandeur only exists in the space of that
which is _not_ grand. The soul, therefore, never con-
demns that which is not grand, but blesses—seeing
_in_ it a _part of itself_ which _must exist_ for another part
of itself to manifest.

The job of the soul, of course, is to cause us to
choose the grandeur—to select the best of Who You
Are—without condemning that which you do not
select.

This is a big task, taking many lifetimes, for you are
wont to rush to judgment, to call a thing "wrong" or
"bad" or "not enough," rather than to bless what you
do not choose.

You do worse than condemn—you actually seek to
do harm to that which you do not choose. You seek to
destroy it. If there is a person, place, or thing with which
you do not agree, you attack it. If there is a religion that
goes against yours, you make it wrong. If there is a
thought that contradicts yours, you ridicule it. If there
is an idea other than yours, you reject it. In this you err,
for you create only half a universe. And you cannot even
understand _your_ half when you have _rejected out of
hand_ the other.

This is all very profound—and I thank you. No one has
ever said these things to me. At least, not with such simplicity. And I am trying to understand. Really, I am. Yet some
of this is difficult to grapple with. You seem to be saying, for
instance, that we should love the "wrong" so that we can
know the "right." Are you saying we must embrace the devil,
so to speak?

How else do you heal him? Of course, a real devil does not exist—but I reply to you in the idiom you choose.

Healing is the process of accepting all, then choosing best. Do you understand that? You cannot *choose* to be God if there is nothing else to choose *from*.

Oops, hold it! Who said anything about choosing to *be God*?

The highest feeling is perfect love, is it not?

Yes, I should think so.

And can you find a better description of God?

No, I cannot.

Well, your soul seeks the highest feeling. It seeks to experience—to *be*—perfect love.

It *is* perfect love—and it *knows this*. Yet it wishes to do *more* than *know* it. It wishes to *be* it *in its experience.*

Of *course* you are seeking to be God! What else did you think you were up to?

I don't know. I'm not sure. I guess I just never thought of it that way. There just seems to be something vaguely blasphemous about that.

Isn't it interesting that you find nothing blasphemous about seeking to be like the devil, but seeking to be like God offends you—

Now wait minute! Who's seeking to be like the devil?

You are! You *all* are! You've even created religions that tell you that you are born in sin—that you are *sinners at birth*—in order to convince yourselves of your own evil. Yet if I told you you are born of God—that you are pure Gods and Goddesses at birth—_pure love_—you would reject me.

All your life you have spent convincing yourself that you are bad. Not only that you are bad, but that the things you want are bad. Sex is bad, money is bad, joy is bad, power is bad, having a lot is bad—a lot _of anything_. Some of your religions have even got you believing that _dancing_ is bad, _music_ is bad, celebrating _life_ is bad. Soon you'll agree that smiling is bad, laughing is bad, _loving_ is bad.

No, no, my friend, you may not be very clear about many things, but about one thing you _are_ clear: you, and most of what you desire, are _bad_. Having made this judgment about yourself, you have decided that your job is to _get better_.

It's okay, mind you. It's the same destination in any event—it's just that there's a faster way, a shorter route, a quicker path.

Which is?

Acceptance of Who and What You Are right now—and demonstration of that.

This is what Jesus did. It is the path of the Buddha, the way of Krishna, the walk of every Master who has appeared on the planet.

And every Master has likewise had the same message: What I am, you are. What I can do, you can do. These things, and _more_, shall you also do.

Yet you have not listened. You have chosen instead the far more difficult path of _one who thinks he is the devil_, one who _imagines he is evil_.

You say it is difficult to walk the path of Christ, to follow the teachings of the Buddha, to hold the light of Krishna, to be a Master. Yet I tell you this: it is far more difficult to _deny_ Who You Are than to accept it.

You are goodness and mercy and compassion and understanding. You are peace and joy and light. You are forgiveness and patience, strength and courage, a helper in time of need, a comforter in time of sorrow, a healer in time of injury, a teacher in times of confusion. You are the deepest wisdom and the highest truth; the greatest peace and the grandest love. You *are* these things. And in moments of your life you have *known* yourself as these things.

Choose now to know yourself as these things always.

4

Whew! You inspire me!

Well, if God can't inspire you, who in hell can?

Are You always this flip?

I meant that not as a flippancy. Read it again.

Oh. I see.

Yes.
However, it would be okay if I were being flip, wouldn't it?

I don't know. I'm used to my God being a little more serious.

Well, do Me a favor, and don't try to contain Me. By the way, do yourself the same favor.
It just so happens I have a great sense of humor. I'd say you'd have to when you see what you've all done with life, wouldn't you? I mean, sometimes I have to just laugh at it.
It's alright, though, because you see, I know it'll all come out all right in the end.

What do You mean by that?

I mean you can't lose in this game. You can't go wrong. It's not part of the plan. There's no way not to get where you are going. There's no way to miss your destination. If God is your target, you're in luck, because *God is so big, you can't miss.*

That's the big worry, of course. The big worry is that somehow we'll mess up and not get to ever see You, be with You.

You mean "get to heaven"?

Yes. We're all afraid of going to hell.

So you've placed yourself there to begin with in order to avoid *going* there. Hmmmmm. Interesting strategy.

There You are, being flip again.

I can't help it. This whole hell thing brings out the worst in Me!

Good grief, You're a regular *comedian.*

It took you this long to find *that* out? You looked at the world lately?

Which brings me to another question. Why don't You *fix* the world, instead of allowing it to go to hell?

Why don't you?

I don't have the power.

Nonsense. You've the power and the ability right now to end world hunger this minute, to cure diseases this instant. What if I told you your own medical profession *holds back* cures, refuses to approve alternative medicines and procedures because they threaten the very structure of the "healing" profession? What if I told you that the governments of the world do not *want* to end world hunger? Would you believe me?

I'd have a hard time with that. I know that's the populist view, but I can't believe it's actually true. No doctor wants to deny a cure. No countryman wants to see his people die.

No *individual* doctor, that's true. No *particular* countryman, that's right. But doctoring and politicking have become *institutionalized,* and it's the institutions that fight these things, sometimes very subtly, sometimes even unwittingly, but inevitably. . .because to those institutions it's a matter of survival.

And so, to give you just one very simple and obvious example, doctors in the West deny the healing efficacies of doctors in the East because to accept them, to admit that certain alternate modalities might just provide some healing, would be to tear at the very fabric of the institution as it has structured itself.

This is not malevolent, yet it is insidious. The profession doesn't do this because it is evil. It does it because it is scared.

All attack is a call for help.

I read that in *A Course in Miracles.*

I put it there.

Boy, You have an answer for everything.

Which reminds Me, we only just started getting to your questions. We were discussing how to get your life on track. How to get it to "take off." I was discussing the process of creation.

Yes, and I kept interrupting.

That's alright, but let's just get back, because we don't want to lose the thread of something that's very important.

Life is a creation, not a discovery.

You do not live each day to *discover* what it holds for you, but to *create* it. You are creating your reality every minute, probably without knowing it.

Here's why that is so, and how that works.

1. I have created you in the image and likeness of God.

2. God is the creator.

3. You are three beings in one. You can call these three aspects of being anything you want: Father, Son, and Holy Ghost; mind, body, and spirit; supoercon- scious, conscious, subconscious.

4. Creation is a process that proceeds from these three parts of your body. Put another way, you create at three levels. The tools of creation are: thought, word, and deed.

5. All creation begins with thought ("Proceeds from the Father"). All creation then moves to word ("Ask and you shall receive, speak and it shall be done unto you"). All creation is fulfilled in deed ("And the Word was made flesh, and dwelt among us").

6. That which you think of, but thereafter never speak of, creates at one level. That which you think of and speak of creates at another level. That which you think, speak, and do becomes made manifest in your reality.

7. To think, speak, and do something which you do not truly believe is impossible. Therefore, the process of creation must include belief, or knowing. This is absolute faith. This is *beyond* hoping. This is *knowing of a certainty* ("By your faith shall ye be healed"). There- fore, the doing part of creation always includes know- ing. It is a gut-level clarity, a total certainty, a complete *acceptance as reality* of something.

8. This place of knowing is a place of intense and incredible gratitude. It is a *thankfulness in advance.* And that, perhaps, is the biggest key to creation: to be grateful *before,* and for, the creation. Such taking for granted is not only condoned, but encouraged. It is the *sure sign of mastery.* All Masters *know in advance that the deed has been done.*

9. Celebrate and enjoy all that you create, have

created. To reject any part of it is to reject a part of yourself. Whatever it is that is now presenting itself as part of your creation, own it, claim it, bless it, be thankful for it. Seek not to condemn it ("God damn it!"), for to condemn it is to condemn yourself.

10. If there is some aspect of creation you find you do not enjoy, bless it and simply change it. Choose again. Call forth a new reality. Think a new thought. Say a new word. Do a new thing. Do this magnificently and the rest of the world will follow you. Ask it to. Call for it to. _Say,_ "I am the Life and the Way, follow me."

This is how to manifest God's will "on Earth as it is in Heaven."

If it is all as simple as that, if these ten steps are all we need, why does it not work that way for more of us?

It _does_ work that way, for _all_ of you. Some of you are using the "system" consciously, with full awareness, and some of you are using it unconsciously, without even knowing what you are doing.

Some of you are walking in wakefulness, and some of you are sleepwalking. Yet _all_ of you are creating your reality—_creating,_ not _discovering_—using the power I have given you, and the process I've just described.

So, you've asked when your life will "take off," and I've given you the answer.

You get your life to "take off" by first becoming very clear in your thinking about it. Think about what you want to be, do, and have. Think about it often until you are very clear about this. Then, when you are very clear, _think about nothing else._ Imagine no other possibilities.

Throw all negative thoughts out of your mental constructions. Lose all pessimism. Release all doubts. Reject all fears. Discipline your mind to hold fast to the original creative thought.

When your thoughts are clear and steadfast, begin to speak them as truths. Say them out loud. Use the great command that calls forth creative power: I am. Make I-am statements to others. "I am" is the strongest creative statement in the universe. Whatever you think, whatever you say, after the words "I am" sets into motion those experiences, calls them forth, brings them to you.

There is no other way the universe knows how to work. There is no other route it knows to take. The universe responds to "I am" as would a genie in a bottle.

You say "Release all doubts, reject all fears, lose all pessimism" as if you're saying "pick me up a loaf of bread." But these things are easier said than done. "Throw all negative thoughts out of your mental constructions" might as well read "climb Mt. Everest—before lunch." It's rather a large order.

Harnessing your thoughts, exercising control over them, is not as difficult as it might seem. (Neither, for that matter, is climbing Mt. Everest.) It is all a matter of discipline. It is a question of intent.

The first step is learning to monitor your thoughts; to *think about* what you are thinking about.

When you catch yourself thinking negative thoughts—thoughts that negate your highest idea about a thing—think again! I want you to do this, *literally*. If you think you are in a doldrum, in a pickle, and no good can come of this, *think again*. If you think the world is a bad place, filled with negative events, *think again*. If you think your life is falling apart, and it looks as if you'll never get it back together again, *think again*.

You *can* train yourself to do this. (Look how well you've trained yourself *not* to do it!)

Thank you. I've never had the process set out for me so clearly. I wish it were as easily done as said— but now I at least understand it clearly—I think.

Well, if you need a review, we have several lifetimes.

5

What is the true path to God? Is it through renunciation, as some yogis believe? And what of this thing called suffering? Is suffering and service the path to God as many ascetics say? Do we earn our way to heaven by "being good," as so many religions teach? Or are we free to act as we wish, violate or ignore any rule, set aside any traditional teachings, dive into any self-indulgences, and thus find Nirvana, as many New Agers say? Which is it? Strict moral standards, or do-as-you-please? Which is it? Traditional values, or make-it-up-as-you-go-along? Which is it? The Ten Commandments, or the Seven Steps to Enlightenment?

> You have a great need to have it be one way or the other, don't you. . .Could it not be all of these?

I don't know. I'm asking You.

> I will answer you, then, as you can best under-stand—though I tell you now that your answer is within. I say this to all people who hear My words and seek My Truth.
>
> Every heart which earnestly asks, Which is the path to God? is shown. Each is given a heartfelt Truth. Come to Me along the path of your heart, not through a journey of your mind. You will never find Me in your mind.
>
> *In order to truly know God, you have to be out of your mind.*
>
> Yet your question begs an answer, and I will not step aside from the thrust of your inquiry.
>
> I will begin with a statement that will startle

you—and perhaps offend the sensitivities of many people. *There are no such things as the Ten Command-ments.*

Oh, My God, there aren't?

No, there are not. Who would I command? Myself? And why would such commandments be required? Whatever I want, is. *N'est ce pas?* How is it therefore necessary to command anyone?

And, if I did issue commandments, would they not be automatically kept? How could I wish something to be so so badly that I would command it—and then sit by and watch it not be so?

What kind of a king would do that? What kind of a ruler?

And yet I tell you this: I am neither a king nor a ruler. I am simply—and awesomely—the Creator. Yet the Creator does not rule, but merely creates, creates—and keeps on creating.

I have created you—blessed you—in the image and likeness of Me. And I have made certain promises and commitments to you. I have told you, in plain language, how it will be with you when you become as one with Me.

You are, as Moses was, an earnest seeker. Moses too, as do you now, stood before Me, begging for answers. "Oh, God of My Fathers," he called. "God of my God, deign to show me. Give me a sign, that I may tell my people! How can we know that we are chosen?"

And I came to Moses, even as I have come to you now, with a divine covenant—an everlasting prom-ise—a sure and certain commitment. "How can I be sure?" Moses asked plaintively. "Because I have told you so," I said. "You have the Word of God."

And the Word of God was not a commandment, but a covenant. These, then, are the. . .

TEN COMMITMENTS

You shall *know* that you have taken the path to God, and you shall *know* that you have *found* God, for there will be these signs, these indications, these *changes* in you:

1. You shall love God with all your heart, all your mind, all your soul. And there shall be no other God set before Me. No longer will you worship human love, or success, money, or power, nor any symbol thereof. You will set aside these things as a child sets aside toys. Not because they are unworthy, but because *you have outgrown them.*

And, you shall *know* you have taken the path to God because:

2. You shall not use the name of God in vain. Nor will you call upon Me for frivolous things. You will understand the *power* of words, and of thoughts, and you would not *think of* invoking the name of God in an unGodly manner. You shall not use My name in vain because you *cannot.* For My name—the Great "I Am"—is *never* used in vain (that is, without result), *nor can it ever be.* And when you have found God, you shall *know this.*

And, I shall give you these other signs as well:

3. You shall remember to keep a day for Me, and you shall call it holy. This, so that you do not long stay in your illusion, but cause yourself to remember who and what you are. And then shall you soon call *every* day the Sabbath, and *every* moment holy.

4. You shall honor your mother and your father—and you will *know* you are the Son of God when you honor your Father/Mother God in all that you say or do or think. And even as you so honor the Mother/Father God, and your father and mother on Earth (for they have given you *life*), so, too, will you honor *everyone.*

5. You *know* you have found God when you observe that you will not murder (that is, willfully kill, without cause). For while you will understand that you cannot

end another's life in any event (all life is eternal), you will not choose to terminate any particular incarnation, nor change any life energy from one form to another, without the most sacred justification. Your new reverence for life will cause you to honor *all* life forms—including plants, trees and animals—and to impact them only when it is for the highest good.

And these other signs will I send you also, that you may know you are on the path:

6. You will not defile the purity of love with dishonesty or deceit, for this is adulterous. I promise you, when you have found God, *you shall not commit this adultery.*

7. You will not take a thing that is not your own, nor cheat, nor connive, nor harm another to have any thing, for this would be to steal. I promise you, when you have found God, *you shall not steal.*

Nor shall you. . .

8. Say a thing that is not true, and thus bear false witness.

Nor shall you. . .

9. Covet your neighbor's spouse, for why would you want your *neighbor's* spouse when you know *all* others are your spouse?

10. Covet your neighbor's goods, for why would you want your *neighbor's* goods when you know that *all* goods can be yours, and all your goods belong to the world?

You will *know* that you have found the path to God when you see these signs. For I promise that no one who truly seeks God shall any longer do these things. It would be impossible to continue such behaviors.

These are your *freedoms*, not your *restrictions.* These are my *commitments*, not my *commandments.* For God does not order about what God has created—God merely tells God's children: this is how you will know that you are coming home.

Moses asked in earnest—"How may I know? Give me a sign." Moses asked the same question that you ask now. The same question all people everywhere have asked since time began. My answer is likewise eternal. But it has never been, and never will be, a commandment. For who shall I command? And who shall I punish should My commandments not be kept?

There is only Me.

So I don't have to keep the Ten Commandments in order to get to heaven.

There is no such thing as "getting to heaven." There is only a knowing that you are already there. There is an accepting, an understanding, not a working for or a striving.

You cannot go to where you already are. To do that, you would have to leave where you are, and that would defeat the whole purpose of the journey.

The irony is that most people think they have to leave where they are to get to where they want to be. And so they leave heaven in order to _get_ to heaven—and go through hell.

Enlightenment is understanding that there is nowhere to go, nothing to do, and nobody you have to be except exactly who you're being right now.

You are on a journey to nowhere.

Heaven—as you call it—is nowhere. Let's just put some space between the _w_ and the _h_ in that word and you'll see that heaven is now. . .here.

Everyone says that! Everyone says that! It's driving me crazy! If "heaven is now here," how come I don't see that? Why don't I feel that? And why is the world such a mess?

I understand your frustration. It's almost as frustrating trying to understand all this as it is trying to _get_ someone to understand it.

Whoa! Wait a minute! Are you trying to say that God gets frustrated?

Who do you suppose *invented* frustration? And do you imagine that *you* can experience something I cannot?

I tell you this: every experience you have, I have. Do you not see I am experiencing my Self *through you?* What else do you suppose all this is for?

I could not know Myself were it not for You. I *created* you that I might know Who I Am.

Now I would not shatter *all* of your illusions about Me in one chapter—so I will tell you that in My most sublime form, which you call God, I do *not* experience frustration.

Whew! That's better. You scared me there for a minute.

But that's not because I can't. It's simply because I don't choose to. You can make the same choice, by the way.

Well, frustrated or not, I still wonder how it can be that heaven is right here, and I don't experience it.

You cannot experience what you don't know. And you don't know you are in "heaven" right now because you have not experienced it. You see, for you it is a vicious circle. You cannot—have not found a way yet to—experience what you do not know, and you do not know what you have not experienced.

What Enlightenment asks you to do is to know something you have not experienced and thus experience it. Knowing opens the door to experience—and you imagine it is the other way around.

Actually, you know a great deal more than you have experienced. You simply don't know that you know.

You know that there is a God, for instance. But you may not know that you know that. So you keep *waiting around* for the experience. And all the while you keep *having it.* Yet you are having it without knowing—which is like not having it at all.

Boy, we're going around in circles here.

Yes, we are. And instead of going around in circles, perhaps we should be the circle itself. This doesn't have to be a vicious circle. It can be a sublime one.

Is renunciation a part of the truly spiritual life?

Yes, because ultimately all Spirit renounces what is not real, and nothing in the life you lead is real, save your relationship with Me. *Yet renunciation in the classic sense of self-denial is not required.*

A true Master does not "give up" something. A true Master simply sets it aside, as he would do with anything for which he no longer has any use.

There are those who say you must overcome your desires. I say you must simply change them. The first practice feels like a rigorous discipline, the second, a joyful exercise.

There are those who say that to know God you must overcome all earthly passions. Yet to understand and accept them is enough. *What you resist persists. What you look at disappears.*

Those who seek so earnestly to overcome all earthly passions often work at it so hard that it might be said, *this* has become their passion. They have a "passion for God"; a passion to know Him. But passion is passion, and to trade one for the other does not eliminate it.

Therefore, judge not that about which you feel passionate. Simply notice it, then see if it serves you, given who and what you wish to be.

Remember, you are constantly in the act of creating yourself. You are in every moment deciding who and what you are. You decide this largely through the choices you make regarding who and what you feel passionate about.

Often a person on what you call a spiritual path *looks like* he has renounced all earthly passion, all human desire. What he has done is understand it, see the illusion, and step aside from the passions that do not serve him—all the while loving the illusion for what it has brought to him: the chance to be wholly free.

Passion is the love of turning being into action. It fuels the engine of creation. It changes concepts to experience.

Passion is the fire that drives us to express who we really are. Never deny passion, for that is to deny Who You Are and Who You Truly Want to Be.

The renunciate never denies passion—the renunciate simply denies attachment to results. Passion is a love of doing. Doing is being, *experienced.* Yet what is often created as part of doing? *Expectation.*

To live your life without *expectation*—without the need for specific results—*that* is freedom. That is Godliness. That is how *I* live.

You are not attached to results?

Absolutely not. My joy is in the creating, not in the aftermath. Renunciation is *not* a decision to deny action. Renunciation is a decision to deny a need for a particular *result.* There is a vast difference.

Could you explain what You mean by the statement, "Passion is the love of turning being into action"?

Beingness is the highest state of existence. It is the purest essence. It is the "now-not now," the "all-not all," the "always-never" aspect of God.

Pure being is pure God-ing.

Yet it has never been enough for us to simply *be.* We have always yearned to *experience* What We Are—and that requires a whole other aspect of divinity, called doing.

Let us say that you are, at the core of your wonderful Self, that aspect of divinity called love. (This is, by the way, the Truth of you.)

Now it is one thing to *be* love—and quite another thing to *do something loving*. *The soul longs to do something about what it is, in order that it might know itself in its own experience. So it will seek to realize its highest idea through action.*

This urge to do this is called passion. Kill passion and you kill God. Passion is God wanting to say "hi."

But, you see, once God (or God-in-you) does that loving thing, God has realized Itself, and needs nothing more.

Man, on the other hand, often feels he needs a *return* on his investment. If we're going to love somebody, fine—but we'd better get some love back. That sort of thing.

This is *not* passion. This is *expectation*.

This is the greatest source of man's unhappiness. It is what separates man from God.

The renunciate seeks to end this separation through the experience some Eastern mystics have called *samadhi*. That is, oneness and union with God; a melding with and melting into divinity.

The renunciate therefore *renounces results*—but never, *ever* renounces passion. Indeed, the Master knows intuitively that passion is the path. It is the way to Self realization.

Even in earthly terms it can be fairly said that if you have a passion for nothing, you have no life at all.

You have said that "what you resist persists, and what you look at disappears." Can You explain that?

You cannot resist something to which you grant no reality. The act of resisting a thing is the act of granting it life. When you resist an energy, you place it there. The more you resist, the more you make it real—*whatever* it is you are resisting.

What you open your eyes and look at disappears. That is, *it ceases to hold its illusory form.*

If you look at something—truly *look* at it—you will see *right through it,* and right through any illusion it holds for you, leaving nothing but ultimate reality in your sight. In the face of ultimate reality your puny illusion has no power. It cannot long hold you in its weakening grip. You see the *truth* of it, and the truth sets you free.

But what if you don't *want* the thing you are looking at to disappear?

You should *always* want it to! There is nothing in your reality to hold onto. Yet if you *do choose* the illusion of your life over ultimate reality, you may simply *recreate it*—just as you created it to begin with. In this way you may have in your life what you *choose to have* and eliminate from your life what you no longer wish to experience.

Yet never resist *anything.* If you think that by your resistance you will eliminate it, *think again.* You only plant it more firmly in place. Have I not told you *all thought* is creative?

Even a thought that says I don't want something?

If you don't want it, why think about it? Don't give it a second thought. Yet if you *must* think about it—that is, if you cannot *not* think about it—then do not resist. Rather, look at whatever it is *directly*—accept the reality as your creation—then choose to keep it or not, as you wish.

What would dictate that choice?

Who and What you think you Are. And Who and What you choose to Be.

This dictates *all* choice—*every* choice you have made in your life. And ever *will* make.

And so the life of a renunciate is an incorrect path?

That is not a truth. The *word* "renunciate" holds such wrongful meaning. In truth, you cannot *renounce anything*—because what you *resist persists*. The true renunciate does not renounce, but simply *chooses differently*. This is an act of moving toward something, not away from something.

You cannot move away from something, because it will chase you all over hell and back. Therefore resist not temptation—but simply turn from it. Turn toward Me and away from anything unlike Me.

Yet know this: there is no such thing as an incorrect path—for on this journey you cannot "not get" where you are going.

It is simply a matter of speed—merely a question of *when* you will get there—yet even that is an illusion, for there is no *"when,"* neither is there a "before" or "after." There is only now; an eternal moment of always in which you are experiencing yourself.

Then what is the point? If there is no way *not* to "get there," what is the point of life? Why should we worry at all about anything we do?

Well, of course, you *shouldn't*. But you *would do well to* be observant. Simply notice who and what you are being, doing, and having, and see whether it serves you.

The point of life is not to get anywhere—it is to notice that you are, and have always been, already there. You are, always and forever, in the moment of pure creation. The point of life is therefore to create—who and what you are, and then to experience that.

6

And what of suffering? Is suffering the way and the path to God? Some say it is the *only* way.

> I am not pleased by suffering, and whoever says I am does not know Me.
>
> Suffering is an unnecessary aspect of the human experience. It is not only unnecessary, it is unwise, uncomfortable, and hazardous to your health.

Then why is there so much suffering? Why don't You, if You *are* God, put an *end* to it if You dislike it so much?

> I have put an end to it. You simply refuse to use the tools I have given you with which to realize that.
>
> You see, suffering has nothing to do with events, but with one's reaction to them.
>
> *What's happening is merely what's happening. How you feel about it is another matter.*
>
> I have given you the tools with which to respond and react to events in a way which reduces—in fact, *eliminates*—pain, but you have not used them.

Excuse me, but why not eliminate the *events*?

> A very good suggestion. Unfortunately, I have no control over them.

You have *no control* over events?

> Of course not. Events are occurrences in time and space which you produce out of choice—and I will

never interfere with choices. To do so would be to obviate the very reason I created you. But I've explained all this before.

Some events you produce willfully, and some events you draw to you—more or less unconsciously. Some events—major natural disasters are among those you toss into this category—are written off to "fate."

Yet even "fate" can be an acronym for "from all thoughts everywhere." In other words, the consciousness of the planet.

The "collective consciousness."

Precisely. Exactly.

There are those who say the world is going to hell in a handbasket. Our ecology is dying. Our planet is in for a major geophysical disaster. Earthquakes. Volcanoes. Maybe even a tilting of the Earth on its axis. And there are others who say collective consciousness can change all that; that we can save the Earth with our thoughts.

Thoughts put into *action.* If enough people everywhere believe something must be done to help the environment, you *will* save the Earth. But you must work fast. So much damage has already been done, for so long. This will take a major attitudinal shift.

You mean if we don't, we *will* see the Earth—and its inhabitants—destroyed?

I have made the laws of the physical universe clear enough for anyone to understand. There are laws of cause and effect which have been sufficiently outlined to your scientists, physicists, and, through them, to your world leaders. These laws don't need to be outlined once more here.

Getting back to suffering—where did we ever get the idea that suffering was *good*? That the saintly "suffer in silence"?

The saintly *do* "suffer in silence," but that does not mean suffering is good. The students in the school of Mastery suffer in silence because they understand that suffering is not the way of God, but rather a sure sign that there is still something to *learn* of the way of God, still something to remember.

The *true Master* does not suffer in silence at all, but only appears to be suffering without complaint. The reason that the true Master does not complain is that the true Master is *not suffering*, but simply experiencing a set of circumstances that *you* would call insufferable.

A practicing Master does not speak of suffering simply because a Master practicing *clearly understands* the *power of the Word*—and so chooses to simply *not say a word about it.*

We make real that to which we pay attention. The Master knows this. The Master places himself *at choice* with regard to that which she chooses to make real.

You have all done this from time to time. There is not a one among you who has not made a headache disappear, or a visit to the dentist less painful, *through your decision about it.*

A Master simply makes the same decision about larger things.

But why have suffering at all? Why have even the *possibility* of suffering?

You cannot know, and become, that which you are, in the absence of that which you are not, as I have already explained to you.

I still don't understand how we ever got the idea that suffering was *good.*

You are wise to be insistent in questioning that. The original wisdom surrounding suffering in silence has become so perverted that now many believe (and several religions actually *teach*) that suffering is *good*, and *joy* is *bad*. Therefore, you have decided that if someone has cancer, but keeps it to himself, he is a saint, whereas if someone has (to pick a dynamite topic) robust sexuality, and celebrates it openly, she is a sinner.

Boy, You did pick a dynamite topic. And You cleverly changed the pronoun, too, from male to female. Was that to make a point?

It was to show you your prejudices. You don't like to think of women *having* robust sexuality, much less celebrating it openly.
You would rather see a man dying without a whimper on the battlefield than a woman making love with a whimper in the street.

Wouldn't *You*?

I have no judgment one way or the other. But you have all sorts of them—and I suggest that it is your judgments which keep you from joy, and your expectations which make you unhappy.
All of this put together is what causes you dis-ease, and therein begins your suffering.

How do I know that what You are saying is true? How do I know this is even God speaking, and not my overactive imagination?

You've asked that before. My answer is the same. What difference does it make? Even if everything I've said is "wrong," can you think of a better way to live?

No.

Then "wrong" is _right_, and "right" is wrong!

Yet I'll tell you this, to help you out of your dilemma: believe _nothing_ I say. Simply _live_ it. _Experience_ it. Then live whatever other paradigm you want to construct. Afterward, look to your _experience_ to find your truth.

One day, if you have a great deal of courage, you will experience a world where making love _is_ considered better than making war. On that day will you rejoice.

7

Life is so scary. And so confusing. I wish things could be more clear.

There is nothing scary about life, if you are not attached to results.

You mean if you don't want anything.

That's right. *Choose*, but don't want.

That's easy for people who don't have anybody depending on them. What if you have a wife and children?

The path of the householder has always been a most challenging path. Perhaps *the* most challenging. As you point out, it is easy to "want nothing" when you are only dealing with yourself. It is natural, when you have others you love, to want only the best for them.

It hurts when you can't give them all that you want them to have. A nice home, some decent clothes, enough food. I feel as though I've been struggling for 20 years just to make ends meet. And I still have nothing to show for it.

You mean in terms of material wealth?

I mean in terms of just some of the basics that a man would like to pass on to his children. I mean in terms of some of the very simple things a man would like to provide for his wife.

I see. You see it as your job in life to provide all these things. Is that what you imagine your life to be about?

I'm not sure I'd state it that way. This is not what my life is *about*, but it sure would be nice if this could be a *by-product*, at least.

Well, let's go back, then. What *do* you see your life being about?

That's a good question. I've had a lot of different answers to that through the years.

What is your answer now?

It feels as though I have two answers to that question; the answer I'd *like* to see, and the answer I'm seeing.

What's the answer you'd *like* to see?

I'd like to see my life being about the evolution of my soul. I'd like to see my life being about expressing and experiencing the part of me I love most. The part of me that is compassion and patience and giving and helping. The part of me that is knowing and wise, forgiving and. . .love.

Sounds like you've been reading this book!

Yes, well it's a beautiful book, on an esoteric level, but I'm trying to figure out how to "practicalize" that. The answer to your question that I see being real in my life is that it's about day-to-day survival.

Oh. And you think one thing precludes the other?

Well. . .

You think esoterics preclude survival?

The truth is, I'd like to do more than just survive. I've been *surviving* all these years. I notice I'm still here. But I'd like the *struggle* for survival to end. I see that just getting by from day to day is still a struggle. I'd like to do more than just survive. I'd like to *prosper*.

And what would you call prospering?

Having enough that I don't have to worry where my next dollar is coming from; not having to stress and strain just to make the rent, or handle the phone bill. I mean, I hate to get so mundane, but we're talking *real life* here, not the airy-fairy, spiritually romanticized picture of life you draw throughout this book.

Do I hear a little anger there?

Not anger so much as frustration. I've been at the spiritual game for over 20 years now, and look where it's gotten me. One paycheck away from the poorhouse! And now I've just lost my job, and it looks like the cash flow has stopped *again*. I'm getting really tired of the struggle. I'm 49 years old, and I'd like to have some *security* in life so that I *could* devote more time to "God stuff," to soul "evoluting," etc. That's where my heart is, but it's not where my life allows me to go. . .

Well, you've said a mouthful there, and I suspect you're speaking for a whole lot of people when you share that experience.

I'm going to respond to your truth one sentence at a time, so that we can easily track, and dissect, the answer.

You have not been "at this spiritual game" for 20 years, you have been barely skirting the edges of it. (This is not a "spanking," by the way, this is just a statement of the truth.) I'll concede that for two decades you've been *looking* at it; *flirting* with it; *experimenting* now and then. . .but I haven't felt your true—your truest—

commitment to the game until just recently.

Let's be clear that *"being at the spiritual game"* means *dedicating your whole mind, your whole body, your whole soul to the process of creating Self in the image and likeness of God.*

This is the process of Self realization about which Eastern mystics have written. It is the process of salvation to which much Western theology has devoted itself.

This is a day-to-day, hour-to-hour, moment-to-moment act of supreme consciousness. It is a choosing and a re-choosing every instant. It is ongoing creation. *Conscious* creation. Creation with a *purpose*. It is using the tools of creation we have discussed, and using them with awareness and sublime intention.

That is "playing this spiritual game." Now, how long have you been at this?

I haven't even begun.

Don't go from one extreme to the other, and don't be so hard on yourself. You *have* been dedicated to this process—and you're actually engaged in it more than you'll give yourself credit for. But you haven't been doing so for 20 years—or anything close to that. Yet the truth is, how long you have been engaged in it is not important. Are you engaged in it *now*? That's all that matters.

Let's move on with your statement. You ask us to "look where it's gotten you," and you describe yourself as being "one step away from the poorhouse." I look at you and see a quite different thing. I see a person who is one step away from the rich house! You feel you are one paycheck from oblivion, and I see you as one paycheck from Nirvana. Now much depends, of course, on what you see as your "pay"—and to what end you are working.

If the object of your life is to acquire what you call security, I see and understand why you feel you are "one paycheck from the poorhouse." Yet even this assessment is open to correction. Because with My pay, *all* good things come to you—including the experience of feeling secure in the physical world.

My pay—the payoff you get when you "work for" Me—provides a great deal more than spiritual comfort. *Physical* comfort, too, can be yours. Yet the ironic part about all this is that, once you experience the kind of spiritual comfort My payoff provides, the last thing you'll find yourself worrying about is physical comfort.

Even the physical comfort of members of your family will no longer be a concern to you—for once you rise to a level of God consciousness you will understand that you are not responsible for any other human soul, and that while it is commendable to wish every soul to live in comfort, each soul must choose—*is choosing*—its own destiny this instant.

Clearly, it is not the highest action to deliberately abuse or destroy another. Clearly, it is equally inappropriate to neglect the needs of those you have caused to be dependent on you.

Your job is to render them *independent;* to teach them as quickly and completely as possible *how to get along without you.* For you are no blessing to them so long as they need you to survive, but bless them truly only in the moment they realize you are unnecessary.

In the same sense, God's greatest moment is the moment you realize you *need no God.*

I know, I know. . .this is the antithesis of everything you've ever been taught. Yet your teachers have told you of an angry God, a jealous God, a God who needs to be needed. And that is not a God at all, but a neurotic substitute for that which would be a deity.

A true Master is not the one with the most students, but one who creates the most Masters.

A true leader is not the one with the most followers, but one who creates the most leaders.

A true king is not the one with the most subjects, but one who leads the most to royalty.

A true teacher is not the one with the most knowledge, but one who causes the most others to have knowledge.

And a true God is not One with the most servants, but One who serves the most, thereby making Gods of all others.

For this is both the goal and the glory of God: that His subjects shall be no more, and that all shall know God not as the unattainable, but as the unavoidable.

I would that you could this understand: your happy destiny is *unavoidable*. You cannot *not* be "saved." There is no hell except not knowing this.

So now, as parents, spouses, and loved ones, seek not to make of your love a glue that binds, but rather a magnet that first attracts, then turns around and repels, lest those who are attracted begin to believe they must stick to you to survive. Nothing could be further from the truth. Nothing could be more damaging to another.

Let your love *propel* your beloveds into the world—and into the full experience of who they are. In this will you have truly loved.

It is a great challenge, this path of the householder. There are many distractions, many worldly concerns. The ascetic is bothered by none of these. He is brought his bread and water, and given his humble mat on which to lie, and he can devote his every hour to prayer, meditation, and contemplation of the divine. How easy to see the divine under such circumstances! How simple a task! Ah, but give one a spouse, and children! See the divine in a baby who needs changing at 3 A.M. See the divine in a bill that needs paying by the first of the month. Recognize the hand of God in the illness that takes a spouse, the job that's lost, the child's fever, the parent's pain. Now we are talking saintliness.

I understand your fatigue. I know you are tired of the struggle. Yet I tell you this: When you follow Me, the struggle disappears. Live in your God space and the events become blessings, one and all.

How can I get to my God space when I've lost my job, the rent needs paying, the kids need a dentist, and being in my lofty, philosophical space seems the least likely way to solve any of this?

Do not forsake Me when you need Me most. Now is the hour of your greatest testing. Now is the time of your greatest chance. It is the chance to prove everything that has been written here.

When I say "don't forsake Me," I sound like that needy, neurotic God we talked about. But I'm not. You can "forsake Me" all you want. I don't care, and it won't change a thing between us. I merely say this in answer to your questions. It is when the going gets tough that you so often forget *Who You Are*, and the *tools* I have given you for creating the life that you would choose.

Now is the time to *go* to your God space more than ever. First, it will bring you great peace of mind—and from a peaceful mind do great ideas flow—ideas which could be solutions to the biggest problems you imagine yourself to have.

Second, it is in your God space that you Self realize, and that is the purpose—the *only* purpose—of your soul.

When you are in your God space, you know and understand that all you are now experiencing is temporary. I tell you that heaven and Earth shall pass away, but *you* shall not. This ever-lasting perspective helps you to see things in their proper light.

You can define these present conditions and circumstances as what they truly are: temporary and temporal. You may then use them as tools—for that is what they are, temporary, temporal tools—in the creation of present experience.

Just who do you think you are? In relationship to the experience called lose-a-job, who do you think you are? And, perhaps more to the point, who do you think *I* am? Do you imagine this is too big a problem for Me to

solve? Is getting out of this jam too big a miracle for Me
to handle? I understand that you may think it's too big
for *you* to handle, even with all the tools I have given
you—but do you really think it's too big for Me?

I know intellectually that no job is too big for God. But
emotionally I guess I can't be sure. Not whether You *can* handle
it, but whether You *will*.

I see. So it's a matter of faith.

Yes.

You don't question My ability, you merely doubt My
desire.

You see, I still live this theology that says there may be a
lesson in here somewhere for me. I'm still not sure I'm
supposed to have a solution. Maybe I'm supposed to have
the *problem*. Maybe this is one of those "tests" my theology
keeps telling me about. So I worry that this problem may *not*
be solved. That this is one of those *You're* going to let me
hang here with. . .

Perhaps this is a good time to go over once more
how it is that I interact with you, because you think it is
a question of My desire, and I'm telling you it's a
question *of yours*.

I want for you what *you* want for you. Nothing more,
nothing less. I don't sit here and make a judgment,
request by request, whether something should be
granted you.

My law is the law of cause and effect, not the law of
We'll See. There is *nothing* you can't have if you choose
it. Even before you ask, I will have given it to you. Do
you believe this?

No. I'm sorry. I've seen too many prayers go unanswered.

Don't be sorry. Just always stay with the truth—the truth of your experience. I understand that. I honor that. That's okay with Me.

Good, because I *don't* believe that whatever I ask, I get. My life has not been a testimony to that. In fact, I *rarely* get what I ask for. When I do, I consider myself damned lucky.

That's an interesting choice of words. You have an option, it seems. In your life, you can either be damned lucky, or you can be blessing lucky. I'd rather you be blessing lucky—but, of course, I'll never interfere with your decisions.

I tell you this: You *always* get what you create, and you are *always creating*.

I do not make a judgment about the creations that you conjure, I simply empower you to conjure more—and more and more and more. If you don't like what you've just created, *choose again*. My job, as God, is to *always give you that opportunity*.

Now you are telling Me that you haven't always gotten what you've wanted. Yet I am here to tell you that you've *always* gotten what you called forth.

Your Life is always a *result of your thoughts about it—including your obviously creative thought that you seldom get what you choose*.

Now in this present instance you see yourself as the victim of the situation in the losing of your job. Yet the truth is that you no longer chose that job. You stopped getting up in the morning in anticipation, and began getting up with dread. You stopped feeling happy about your work and began feeling resentment. You even began fantasizing *doing something else*.

You think these things mean nothing? You misunderstand your power. I tell you this: *Your Life proceeds out of your* intentions *for it*.

So what is your intention now? Do you intend to prove your theory that life seldom brings you what you choose? Or do you intend to demonstrate Who You Really Are and Who I Am?

I feel chagrined. Chastised. Embarrassed.

Does that serve you? Why not simply acknowledge the truth when you hear it, and move toward it? There is no need to recriminate against yourself. Simply notice what you've been choosing and choose again.

But why am I so ready to always choose the negative? And then to spank myself for it?

What can you expect? You were told from your earliest days that you're "bad." You accept that you were born in "sin." Feeling guilty is a *learned response.* You've been told to feel guilty about yourself for things you did before you could even do anything. You have been taught to feel shame for being born less than perfect.

This alleged state of imperfection in which you are said to have come into this world is what your religionists have the gall to call original sin. And it *is* original sin—but not yours. It is the first sin to be perpetrated upon you by a world which knows nothing of God if it thinks that God would—or *could*—create *anything* imperfect.

Some of your religions have built up whole theologies around this misconception. And that is what it is, *literally*: a *misconception. For anything I conceive—all that to which I give life—is perfect; a perfect reflection of perfection itself, made in the image and likeness of Me.*

Yet, in order to justify the idea of a punitive God, your religions needed to create something for Me to be angry about. So that even those people who lead exemplary lives somehow need to be saved. If they don't need to be saved from themselves, then they need to be saved from their own *built-in imperfection*. So (these religions say) you'd better *do* something about all of this—and fast—or you'll go straight to hell.

This, in the end, may do nothing to mollify a weird, vindictive, angry God, but it does give life to weird, vindictive, angry *religions*. Thus do religions perpetuate themselves. Thus does power remain concentrated in the hands of the few, rather than experienced though the hands of the many.

Of *course* you choose constantly the lesser thought, the smaller idea, the tiniest concept of yourself and your power, to say nothing of Me and Mine. You've been *taught* to.

My God, how can I undo the teaching?

A good question, and addressed to just the right person!

You can undo the teaching by reading and re-reading this book. Over and over again, read it. Until you understand every passage. Until you're familiar with every word. When you can quote its passages to others, when you can bring its phrases to mind in the midst of the darkest hour, then you will have "undone the teaching."

Yet there is still so much I want to ask You; still so much I want to know.

Indeed. You began with a very long list of questions. Shall we get back to it?

8

When will I learn enough about relationships to be able to have them go smoothly? Is there a way to *be* happy in relationships? Must they be constantly challenging?

You have nothing to learn about relationships. You have only to demonstrate what you already know.

There *is* a way to be happy in relationships, and that is to use relationships for their intended purpose, not the purpose you have designed.

Relationships are constantly challenging; constantly calling you to create, express, and experience higher and higher aspects of yourself, grander and grander visions of yourself, ever more magnificent *versions* of yourself. Nowhere can you do this more immediately, impactfully, and immaculately than in relationships. In fact, without relationships, *you cannot do it at all.*

It is *only* through your relationship with other people, places, and events that you can even exist (as a knowable quantity, as an identifiable *something*) in the universe. Remember, absent everything *else*, you are *not.* You only are what you are relative to another thing that is not. That is how it is in the world of the relative, as opposed to the world of the absolute—where I reside.

Once you clearly understand this, once you deeply grasp it, then you intuitively bless each and every experience, all human encounter, and especially personal human relationships, for you see them as constructive, in the highest sense. You see that they can be used, must be used, *are* being used (whether you want them to be or not) to *construct* Who You Really Are.

That construction can be a magnificent creation of your own conscious design, or a strictly happenstance configuration. You can choose to be a person who has resulted simply from what has happened, or from what you've chosen to *be* and *do* about what has happened. It is in the latter form that creation of Self becomes conscious. It is in the second experience that Self becomes realized.

Bless, therefore, *every* relationship, and hold each as special and formative of Who You Are—and now choose to be.

Now your inquiry has to do with individual human relationships of the romantic sort, and I understand that. So let Me address Myself specifically, and at length, to human love relationships—these things which continue to give you such trouble!

When human love relationships fail (relationships never truly fail, except in the strictly human sense that they did not produce what you want), they fail because they were entered into for the wrong reason.

("Wrong," of course, is a relative term, meaning something measured against that which is "right" —whatever *that* is! It would be more accurate in your language to say "relationships fail—change—most often when they are entered into for reasons not wholly beneficial or conducive to their survival.")

Most people enter into relationships with an eye toward what they can get out of them, rather than what they can put into them.

The purpose of a relationship is to decide what part of yourself you'd like to see "show up," not what part of another you can capture and hold.

There can be only one purpose for relationships—and for all of *life:* to be and to decide Who You Really Are.

It is very romantic to say that you were "nothing" until that special other came along, but it is not true. Worse, it puts an incredible pressure on the other to be all sorts of things he or she is not.

Not wanting to "let you down," they try very hard to be and do these things until they cannot anymore. They can no longer complete your picture of them. They can no longer fill the roles to which they have been assigned. Resentment builds. Anger follows.

Finally, in order to save themselves (and the relationship), these special others begin to reclaim their real selves, acting more in accordance with Who They Really Are. It is about this time that you say they've "really changed."

It is very romantic to say that now that your special other has entered your life, you feel complete. Yet the purpose of relationship is not to have another who might complete you; but to have another with whom you might share your completeness.

Here is the paradox of all human relationships: You have no need for a particular other in order for you to experience, fully, Who You Are, and. . .without another, you are nothing.

This is both the mystery and the wonder, the frustration and the joy of the human experience. It requires deep understanding and total willingness to live within this paradox in a way which makes sense. I observe that very few people do.

Most of you enter your relationship-forming years ripe with anticipation, full of sexual energy, a wide-open heart, and a joyful, if eager, soul.

Somewhere between 40 and 60 (and for most it is sooner rather than later) you've given up on your grandest dream, set aside your highest hope, and settled for your lowest expectation—or nothing at all.

The problem is so basic, so simple, and yet so tragically misunderstood: your grandest dream, your highest idea, and your fondest hope has had to do with your beloved other rather than your beloved Self. The test of your relationships has had to do with how well the other lived up to your ideas, and how well you saw yourself living up to his or hers. Yet the only true test has to do with how well you live up to yours.

Relationships are *sacred* because they provide life's grandest opportunity—indeed, its only opportunity—to create and produce the *experience* of your highest conceptualization of Self. Relationships fail when you see them as life's grandest opportunity to create and produce the experience of your highest conceptualization of *another*.

Let each person in relationship worry about *Self*—what *Self* is being, doing, and having; what *Self* is wanting, asking, giving; what *Self* is seeking, creating, experiencing, and all relationships would magnificently serve their purpose—and their participants!

Let each person in relationship worry not about the other, but only, only, only about Self.

This seems a strange teaching, for you have been told that in the highest form of relationship, one worries *only* about the other. Yet I tell you this: your focus upon the other—your *obsession* with the other—is what causes relationships to fail.

What is the other being? What is the other doing? What is the other having? What is the other saying? Wanting? Demanding? What is the other thinking? Expecting? Planning?

The Master understands that it doesn't *matter* what the other is being, doing, having, saying, wanting, demanding. It doesn't *matter* what the other is thinking, expecting, planning. It only matters what *you* are being in *relationship* to that.

The most loving person is the person who is Self-centered.

That *is* a radical teaching. . .

Not if you look at it carefully. If you cannot love your Self, you cannot love another. Many people make the mistake of seeking love of Self *through* love for another. Of course, they don't realize they are doing this. It is not a conscious effort. It's what's going on in the mind. Deep in the mind. In what you call the subconscious.

They think: "If I can just love others, they will love me. Then I will be lovable, and *I* can love me."

The reverse of this is that so many people hate themselves because they feel there is not another who loves them. This is a sickness—it's when people are truly "lovesick" because the truth is, other people *do* love them, but it doesn't matter. No matter how many people profess their love for them, it is not enough.

First, they don't believe you. They think you are trying to manipulate them—trying to get something. (How could you love them for who they truly are? No. There must be some mistake. You must want something! Now what do you want?)

They sit around trying to figure out how anyone could actually love them. So they don't believe you, and embark on a campaign to make you *prove* it. You have to prove that you love them. To do this, they may ask you to start altering your behavior.

Second, if they finally come to a place where they *can* believe you love them, they begin at once to worry about how long they can *keep* your love. So, in order to hold onto your love, they start altering *their* behavior.

Thus, two people literally lose themselves in a relationship. They get into the relationship hoping to find themselves, and they lose themselves instead.

This losing of the Self in a relationship is what causes most of the bitterness in such couplings.

Two people join together in a partnership hoping that the whole will be greater than the sum of the parts, only to find that it's less. They feel *less* than when they were single. Less capable, less able, less exciting, less attractive, less joyful, less content.

This is because they *are* less. They've given up most of who they are in order to be—and to stay—in their relationship.

Relationships were never meant to be this way. Yet this is how they are experienced by more people than you could ever know.

Why? *Why?*

It is because people have lost touch with (if they ever *were* in touch with) the *purpose* of relationships.

When you lose sight of each other as sacred souls on a sacred journey, then you cannot see the purpose, the reason, behind all relationships.

The soul has come to the body, and the body to life, for the purpose of evolution. You are *evolving*, you are *becoming*. And you are using your relationship with *everything* to decide *what* you are becoming.

This is the job you came here to do. This is the joy of creating Self. Of knowing Self. Of becoming, consciously, what you wish to be. It is what is meant by being Self conscious.

You have brought your Self to the relative world so that you might have the tools with which to know and experience Who You Really Are. Who You Are is who you create yourself to be in relationship to all the rest of it.

Your personal relationships are the most important elements in this process. Your personal relationships are therefore holy ground. They have virtually nothing to do with the other, yet, because they involve another, they have *everything* to do with the other.

This is the divine dichotomy. This is the closed circle. So it is not such a radical teaching to say, "Blessed are the Self-centered, for they shall know God." It might not be a bad goal in your life to know the highest part of your Self, and to stay *centered* in that.

Your first relationship, therefore, must be with your Self. You must first learn to honor and cherish and love your Self.

You must first see your Self as worthy before you can see another as worthy. You must first see your Self as blessed before you can see another as blessed. You must first know your Self to be holy before you can acknowledge holiness in another.

If you put the cart before the horse—as most religions ask you to do—and acknowledge another as holy before you acknowledge yourself, you will one day resent it. If there is one thing none of you can tolerate, it is someone being *holier than thou.* Yet your religions force you to call others holier than thou. And so you do it—for a while. Then you crucify them.

You have crucified (in one way or another) all of My teachers, not just One. And you did so not because they were holier than thou, but because you *made them out to be.*

My teachers have all come with the same message. Not "I am holier than thou," but "You are as holy as am I."

This is the message you have not been able to hear; this is the truth you have not been able to accept. And that is why you can never truly, purely, fall in love with another. You have never truly, purely fallen in love with your Self.

And so I tell you this: be now and forever centered upon your Self. Look to see what *you* are being, doing, and having in any given moment, not what's going on with another.

It is not in the action of another, but in your re-action, that your salvation will be found.

I know better, but somehow this makes it sound as though we should not mind what others do to us in relationships. They can do anything, and so long as we hold our equilibrium, keep our Self centered, and all that good stuff, nothing can touch us. But others *do* touch us. Their actions *do* sometimes hurt us. It is when the hurt comes into relationships that I don't know what to do. It's all very well to say "stand aside from it; cause it to mean nothing," but that's easier said than done. I *do* get hurt by the words and actions of others in relationships.

The day will come when you will not. That will be the day on which you realize—and actualize—the true meaning of relationships; the true reason for them.

It is because you have forgotten this that you react

the way you do. But that is alright. That is part of the growth process. It is part of evolution. It is Soul Work you are up to in relationship, yet that is a grand understanding, a grand remembering. Until you remember this—and remember then also how to _use_ relationship as a tool in the creation of Self—you must work at the level at which you are. The level of understanding, the level of willingness, the level of remembrance.

And so there are things you can do when you react with pain and hurt to what another is being, saying, or doing. The first is to admit honestly to yourself and to another exactly how you are feeling. This many of you are afraid to do, because you think it will make you "look bad." Somewhere, deep inside of you, you realize that it probably _is_ ridiculous for you to "feel that way." It probably _is_ small of you. You _are_ "bigger than that." But you can't _help_ it. You still _feel that way_.

There is only one thing you can do. You must honor your feelings. For honoring your feelings means honoring your Self. And you must love your neighbor as you love yourself. How can you ever expect to understand and honor the feelings of another if you cannot honor the feelings within your Self?

The first question in any interactive process with another is: now Who Am I, and Who Do I Want to Be, in relationship to that?

Often you do not remember Who You Are, and do not know Who You Want to Be until you _try out_ a few ways of being. That is why honoring your truest feelings is so important.

If your first feeling is a negative feeling, simply _having the feeling_ is frequently all that is needed to step away from it. It is when you _have_ the anger, _have_ the upset, _have_ the disgust, _have_ the rage, _own_ the feeling of wanting to "hurt back," that you can disown these first feelings as "not Who You Want to Be."

The Master is one who has lived through enough such experiences to know in advance what her final choices are. She does not need to "try out" anything.

She's worn these clothes before and knows they *do not fit;* they are not "her." And since a Master's life is devoted to the constant realization of Self as one *knows oneself to be,* such ill-fitting feelings would never be entertained.

That is why Masters are imperturbable in the face of what others might call calamity. A Master blesses calamity, for the Master knows that from the seeds of disaster (and all experience) comes the growth of Self. And the Master's second life purpose is always *growth.* For once one has fully Self realized, there is *nothing left to do* except *be more of that.*

It is at this stage that one moves from soul work to God work, for this is what *I* am up to!

I will assume for the purposes of this discussion that you are still up to soul work. You are still seeking to realize (make "real") Who You Truly Are. Life (I) will give you bountiful opportunities to create that (remember, life is not a process of discovery, life is a process of creation).

You can create Who You Are over and over again. Indeed, you do—every day. As things now stand, you do not always come up with the same answer, however. Given an identical outer experience, on day one you may choose to be patient, loving, and kind in relationship to it. On day two you may choose to be angry, ugly, and sad.

The Master is one who *always comes up with the same answer*—and that answer is always the *highest choice.*

In this the Master is imminently predictable. Conversely, the student is completely unpredictable. One can tell how one is doing on the road to mastery by simply noticing how predictably one makes the highest choice in responding or reacting to any situation.

Of course, this throws open the question, *what choice is highest?*

That is a question around which have revolved the philosophies and theologies of man since the beginning of time. If the question truly engages you, *you are already on your way to mastery.* For it is still true that most people continue to be engaged by another question altogether. Not, what is the highest choice, but, what is the most profitable? Or, how can I lose the least?

When life is lived from a standpoint of damage control or optimum advantage, the *true* benefit of life is forfeited. The opportunity is lost. The chance is missed. For a life lived thusly is a life lived from fear—and that life speaks a lie about you.

For you are not fear, you are love. Love that needs no protection, love that cannot be lost. Yet you will never know this in your *experience* if you continually answer the second question and not the first. For only a person who thinks there is something *to gain or to lose* asks the second question. And only a person who sees life in a different way; who sees Self as a higher being; who understands that winning or losing is *not* the test, but only loving or failing to love—only that person asks the first.

He who asks the second question says, "I am my body." She who asks the first says, "I am my soul."

Yea, let all those who have ears to hear, listen. For I tell you this: at the critical juncture in all human relationships, there is only one question:

What would love do now?

No other question is relevant, no other question is meaningful, no other question has any importance to your soul.

Now we come upon a very delicate point of interpretation, for this principle of love-sponsored action has been widely misunderstood—and it is this misunderstanding which has led to the resentments and angers of life—which, in turn, have caused so many to stray from the path.

For centuries you have been taught that love-sponsored action arises out of the choice to be, do, and have whatever produces the highest good for another.

Yet I tell you this: the highest choice is that which produces the highest good *for you.*

As with all profound spiritual truth, this statement opens itself to immediate misinterpretation. The mystery clears a bit the moment one decides what *is* the highest "good" one could do for oneself. And when the absolute highest choice is made, the mystery dissolves, the circle completes itself, and the highest good for you *becomes* the highest good for another.

It may take lifetimes to understand this—and even more lifetimes to implement—for this truth revolves around an even greater one: What you do for your Self, you do for another. What you do for another, you do for the Self.

This is because you and the other are one.

And *this* is because. . .

There is naught but You.

All the Masters who have walked your planet have taught this. ("Verily, verily, I say unto you, inasmuch as ye have done it unto one of the least of these my brethren, ye have done it unto Me.") Yet this has remained for most people merely a grand esoteric truth, with *little practical application*. In fact, it is the most practically applicable "esoteric" truth of all time.

It is important in relationships to remember this truth, for without it relationships will be very difficult.

Let's go back to the practical applications of this wisdom and step away from the purely spiritual, esoteric aspect of it for now.

So often, under the old understandings, people—well-meaning and well-intentioned and many very religious—did what they thought would be best for the other person in their relationships. Sadly, all this produced in many cases (in *most* cases) was continued abuse by the other. Continued mistreatment. Continued dysfunction in the relationship.

Ultimately, the person trying to "do what is right" by the other—to be quick to forgive, to show compassion, to continually look past certain problems and behaviors—becomes resentful, angry, and mistrusting, even of God. For how can a just God demand such unending suffering, joylessness, and sacrifice, even in the name of love?

The answer is, God does not. God asks only that you *include yourself* among those you love.

God goes further. God suggests—*recommends*—that you put yourself first.

I do this knowing full well that some of you will call this blasphemy, and therefore not My word, and that others of you will do what might be even worse: *accept it as My word* and misinterpret or distort it to suit your own purposes; to justify unGodly acts.

I tell you this—putting yourself first in the highest sense *never* leads to an unGodly act.

If, therefore, you have caught yourself in an unGodly act as a result of doing what is best for you, the confusion is not in having put yourself first, but rather in misunderstanding what is best for you.

Of course, determining what is best for you will require you to also determine what it is you are trying to do. This is an important step that many people ignore. What are you "up to"? What is your purpose in life? Without answers to these questions, the matter of what is "best" in any given circumstances will remain a mystery.

As a practical matter—again leaving esoterics aside—if you look to what is best for you in these situations where you are being abused, at the very least what you will do is stop the abuse. And that will be good for both you *and* your abuser. *For even an abuser is abused when his abuse is allowed to continue.*

This is not healing to the abuser, but damaging. For if the abuser finds that his abuse is acceptable, what has he learned? Yet if the abuser finds that his abuse will be accepted no more, what has he been allowed to discover?

Therefore, treating others with love does not necessarily mean allowing others to do as they wish.

Parents learn this early with children. Adults are not so quick to learn it with other adults, nor nation with nation.

Yet despots cannot be allowed to flourish, but must be stopped in their despotism. Love of Self, *and love of the despot*, demands it.

This is the answer to your question, "If love is all there is, how can man ever justify war?"

Sometimes man must go to war to make the grandest statement about who man truly is: he who abhors war.

There are times when you may have to *give up* Who You Are in order to *be* Who You Are.

There are Masters who have taught: you cannot *have* it all until you are willing to *give it all up*.

Thus, in order to "have" yourself as a man of peace, you may have to give up the idea of yourself as a man who never goes to war. History has called upon men for such decisions.

The same is true in the most individual and the most personal relationships. Life may more than once call upon you to prove Who You Are by demonstrating an aspect of Who You Are Not.

This is not so difficult to understand if you have lived a few years, though for the idealistically young it may seem the ultimate contradiction. In more mature retrospection it seems more divine dichotomy.

This does not mean in human relationships that if you are being hurt, you have to "hurt back." (Nor does it mean so in relationships between nations.) It simply means that to *allow* another to continually inflict damage may not be the most loving thing to do—for your Self or the other.

This should put to rest some pacifist theories that highest love requires no forceful response to what you consider evil.

The discussion here turns esoteric once more, because no serious exploration of this statement can ignore the word "evil," and the value judgments it invites. In truth, there is nothing evil, only objective phenomena and experience. Yet your very purpose in life requires you to select from the growing collection of endless phenomena a scattered few which you call evil—for unless you do, you cannot call yourself, nor anything else, good—and thus cannot know, or create, your Self.

By that which you call evil do you define your-self—and by that which you call good.

The biggest evil would therefore be to declare nothing evil at all.

You exist in this life in the world of the relative, where one thing can exist only insofar as it relates to another. This is at one and the same time both the function and the purpose of relationship: to provide a field of experience within which you find yourself, define yourself, and—if you choose—constantly recreate Who You Are.

Choosing to be God-like does not mean you choose to be a martyr. And it certainly does not mean you choose to be a victim.

On your way to mastery—when all possibility of hurt, damage, and loss is eliminated—it would be well to recognize hurt, damage, and loss as part of your experience, and decide Who You Are in relationship to it.

Yes, the things that others think, say, or do *will* sometimes hurt you—until they do not anymore. What will get you from here to there most quickly is total honesty—being willing to assert, acknowledge, and declare exactly how you feel about a thing. Say your truth—kindly, but fully and completely. Live your truth, gently, but totally and consistently. Change your truth easily and quickly when your experience brings you new clarity.

No one in right mind, least of all God, would tell you, when you are hurt in a relationship, to "stand aside from it, cause it to mean nothing." If you are *now hurting,* it is too late to cause it to mean nothing. Your task now is to decide what it *does* mean—and to demonstrate that. For in so doing, you choose and become Who You Seek to Be.

So I *don't* have to be the long-suffering wife or the belittled husband or the victim of my relationships in order to render them holy, or to make me pleasing in the eyes of God.

Good grief, of course not.

And I *don't* have to put up with attacks on my dignity, assaults on my pride, damage to my psyche, and wounds to my heart in order to say that I "gave it my best" in a relationship; "did my duty" or "met my obligation" in the eyes of God and man.

Not for one minute.

Then, pray God, tell me—what promises should I make in relationship; what agreements must I keep? What obligations do relationships carry? What guidelines should I seek?

> The answer is the answer you cannot hear—for it leaves you without guidelines and renders null and void every agreement in the moment you make it. The answer is: you have *no* obligation. Neither in relationship, nor in all of life.

No obligation?

> *No* obligation. Nor any restriction or limitation, nor any guidelines or rules. Nor are you bound by any circumstances or situations, nor constrained by any code or law. Nor are you punishable for any offense, nor *capable* of any—for there is no such thing as being "offensive" in the eyes of God.

I've heard this before—this "there are no rules" kind of religion. That's spiritual anarchy. I don't see how that can work.

> There is no way it *cannot* work—if you are about the business of creating your Self. If, on the other hand, you imagine yourself to be about the task of trying to be what someone *else* wants you to be, the absence of rules or guidelines might indeed make things difficult.

Yet the thinking mind begs to ask: if God has a way She wants me to be, why didn't She simply *create me that way to begin with?* Why all this struggle for me to "overcome" who I am in order for me to become what God wants me to be? This the probing mind demands to know—and rightly so, for it is a proper inquiry.

The religionists would have you believe that I created you as less than Who I Am so that you could have the chance to *become* as Who I Am, working against all odds—and, I might add, against *every natural tendency I am supposed to have given you.*

Among these so-called natural tendencies is the tendency to sin. You are taught that you were *born* in sin, that you will *die* in sin, and that to sin is your *nature.*

One of your religions even teaches you that you *can do nothing about this.* Your own actions are irrelevant and meaningless. It is arrogant to think that by some action of *yours* you can "get to heaven." There is only *one* way to heaven (salvation) and that is through no undertaking of your own, but through the grace granted you by God through acceptance of His Son as your intermediary.

Once this is done you are "saved." Until it is done, nothing that you do—not the life you live, not the choices you make, not anything you undertake of your own will in an effort to improve yourself or render you worthy—has any effect, bears any influence. You are *incapable* of rendering yourself worthy, because you are inherently unworthy. You were *created* that way.

Why? God only knows. Perhaps He made a mistake. Perhaps He didn't get it right. Maybe He wishes He could have it all to do over again. But there it is. What to do. . .

You're making mock of me.

No. You are making mock of Me. You are saying that I, God, made inherently imperfect beings, then have demanded of them to be perfect, or face damnation.

136

You are saying then that, somewhere several thousand years into the world's experience, I relented, saying that from then on you didn't necessarily *have* to be good, you simply had to feel bad when you were not being good, and accept as your savior the One Being who could *always* be perfect, thus satisfying My hunger for perfection. You are saying that My Son—who you call the One Perfect One—has saved you from your own imperfection—the imperfection *I gave you*.

In other words, God's Son has saved you from *what His Father did*.

This is how you—many of you—say I've set it up.

Now *who is mocking whom?*

That is the second time in this book you seem to have launched a frontal attack on fundamentalist Christianity. I am surprised.

You have chosen the word "attack." I am simply engaging the issue. And the issue, by the way, is not "fundamentalist Christianity," as you put it. It is the entire nature of God, and of God's relationship to man.

The question comes up here because we were discussing the matter of obligations—in relationships and in life itself.

You cannot believe in an obligation-less relationship because you cannot accept who and what you really are. You call a life of complete freedom "spiritual anarchy." I call it God's great promise.

It is only within the context of this promise that God's great plan can be completed.

You have *no* obligation in relationship. You have only opportunity.

Opportunity, not obligation, is the cornerstone of religion, the basis of all spirituality. So long as you see it the other way around, you will have missed the point.

Relationship—your relationship to all things—was created as your perfect tool in the work of the soul. That is why all human relationships are sacred ground. It is why every personal relationship is holy.

In this, many churches have it right. Marriage *is* a sacrament. But not because of its sacred obligations. Rather, because of its unequalled opportunity.

Never do anything in relationship out of a sense of obligation. Do whatever you do out of a sense of the glorious opportunity your relationship affords you to decide, and to be, Who You Really Are.

I can hear that—yet over and over in my relationships I have given up when the going gets tough. The result is that I've had a string of relationships where I thought, as a kid, that I'd have only one. I don't seem to know what it's like to hold onto a relationship. Do you think I will ever learn? What do I have to do to make it happen?

You make it sound as if holding onto a relationship means it's been a success. Try not to confuse longevity with a job well done. Remember, your job on the planet is not to see how long you can stay in relationship, it's to decide, and experience, Who You Really Are.

This is not an argument for *short*-term relationships— yet neither is there a requirement for long-term ones.

Still, while there is no such requirement, this much should be said: long-term relationships do hold remarkable opportunities for *mutual* growth, *mutual* expression, and *mutual* fulfillment—and that has its own reward.

I know, I know! I mean, I've always suspected that. So how do I get there?

First, make sure you get into a relationship for the right reasons. (I'm using the word "right" here as a relative term. I mean "right" relative to the larger purpose you hold in your life.)

As I have indicated before, most people still enter relationships for the "wrong" reasons—to end loneliness, fill a gap, bring themselves love, or someone *to* love—and those are some of the *better* reasons. Others do so to salve their ego, end their depressions, improve their sex life, recover from a previous relationship, or, believe it or not, to relieve boredom.

None of these reasons will work, and unless something dramatic changes along the way, neither will the relationship.

I didn't enter into my relationships for any of those reasons.

I would challenge that. I don't think you know why you entered your relationships. I don't think you thought about it in this way. I don't think you entered your relationships purposefully. I think you entered your relationships because you "fell in love."

That's exactly right.

And I don't think you stopped to look at why you "fell in love." What was it to which you were responding? What need, or set of needs, was being fulfilled?

For most people, love is a response to need fulfillment.

Everyone has needs. You need this, another needs that. You both see in each other a chance for *need fulfillment.* So you agree—tacitly—to a trade. I'll trade you what I've got if you'll give me what you've got.

It's a transaction. But you don't tell the truth about it. You don't say, "I trade you very much." You say, "I love you very much," and then the disappointment begins.

You've made this point before.

Yes, and you've *done* this thing before—not once, but several times.

Sometimes this book seems to be going in circles, making the same points over and over again.

Sort of like life.

Touché.

> The process here is that you're asking the questions and I'm merely answering them. If you ask the same question three different ways, I'm obliged to continue answering it.

Maybe I keep hoping You'll come up with a different answer. You take a lot of the romance out of it when I ask You about relationships. What's *wrong* with falling head over heels in love without having to *think* about it?

> Nothing. Fall in love with as many people as you like that way. *But if you're going to form a lifelong relationship with them, you may want to add a little thought.*
> On the other hand, if you enjoy going through relationships like water—or, worse yet, staying in one because you think you "have to," then living a life of quiet desperation—if you enjoy repeating these patterns from your past, keep right on doing what you've been doing.

Okay, okay. I get it. Boy, You're relentless, aren't You?

> That's the problem with truth. The *truth* is relentless. It won't leave you alone. It keeps creeping up on you from every side, showing you what's really so. That can be annoying.

Okay. So I want to find the tools for a long-term relationship—and you say entering relationships purposefully is one of them.

Yes. Be sure you and your mate agree on purpose.

If you both agree at a conscious level that the purpose of your relationship is to create an opportunity, not an obligation—an opportunity for growth, for full Self expression, for lifting your lives to their highest potential, for healing every false thought or small idea you ever had about you, and for ultimate reunion with God through the communion of your two souls—if you take that vow instead of the vows you've been taking—the relationship has begun on a very good note. It's gotten off on the right foot. That's a very good beginning.

Still, it's no guarantee of success.

If you want guarantees in life, then you don't want life. *You want rehearsals for a script that's already been written.*

Life by its nature cannot *have guarantees, or its whole purpose is thwarted.*

Okay. Got it. So now I've got my relationship off to this "very good start." Now, how do I keep it going?

Know and understand that there will be challenges and difficult times.

Don't try to avoid them. Welcome them. Gratefully. See them as grand gifts from God; glorious opportunities to do what you came into the relationship—and life—*to do.*

Try very hard not to see your partner as the enemy, or the opposition, during these times.

In fact, seek to see no one, and nothing, as the enemy—or even the problem. Cultivate the technique of seeing all problems as opportunities. Opportunities to. . .

. . .I know, I know—"be, and decide, Who You Really Are."

Right! You're getting it! You *are* getting it!

Sounds like a pretty dull life to me.

Then you're setting your sights too low. Broaden the scope of your horizons. Extend the depth of your vision. See more in you than you think there is to be seen. See more in your partner, too.

You will never disserve your relationship—nor anyone—by seeing more in another than they are showing you. For there is more there. Much more. It is only their fear that stops them from showing you. If others notice that you see them as more, they will feel safe to show you what you obviously already see.

People tend to live up to our expectations of them.

Something like that. I don't like the word "expectations" here. Expectations *ruin* relationships. Let's say that people tend to see in themselves what we see in them. The grander our vision, the grander their willingness to access and display the part of them *we have shown them*.

Isn't that how all truly blessed relationships work? Isn't that part of the healing process—the process by which we give people permission to "let go" of every false thought they've ever had about themselves?

Isn't that what I am doing *here*, in this book, for *you*?

Yes.

And that is the work of God. The work of the soul is to wake yourself up. The work of God is to wake everybody *else* up.

We do this by seeing others as Who They Are—by reminding them of Who They Are.

This you can do in two ways—by reminding them of Who They Are (very difficult, because they will not believe you), and by remembering Who You Are (much easier, because you do not need *their* belief, only your own). Demonstrating this constantly ultimately reminds others of Who They Are, for they will see themselves in you.

Many Masters have been sent to the Earth to demonstrate Eternal Truth. Others, such as John the Baptist, have been sent as messengers, telling of the Truth in glowing terms, speaking of God with unmistakable clarity.

These special messengers have been gifted with extraordinary insight, and the very special power to see and receive Eternal Truth, plus the ability to communicate complex concepts in ways that can and will be understood by the masses.

You are such a messenger.

I am?

Yes. Do you believe this?

It is such a difficult thing to accept. I mean, all of us want to be special. . .

. . .all of you *are* special. . .

. . .and the ego gets in there—at least with *me* it does, and tries to make us feel somehow "chosen" for an amazing assignment. I have to fight that ego all the time, seek to purify and re-purify my every thought, word, and deed so as to keep personal aggrandizement out of it. So it's very difficult to hear what you're saying, because I'm aware that it plays to my ego, and I've spent all my life fighting my ego.

I know you have.
And sometimes not too successfully.

I am chagrined to have to agree.

Yet always when it has come to God, you have let the ego drop. Many is the night you have begged and pleaded for clarity, beseeched the heavens for insight, not so that you could enrich yourself, or heap honor upon yourself, but out of the deep purity of a simple yearning to *know*.

Yes.

And you have promised Me, over and over again, that should you be caused to know, you would spend the rest of your life—every waking moment—sharing Eternal Truth with others. . .not out of a need to gain glory, but out of your heart's deepest desire to end the pain and suffering of others; to bring joy and gladness, and help and healing; to reconnect others with the sense of partnership with God you have always experienced.

Yes. Yes.

And so I have chosen you to be My messenger. You, and many others. For now, during these times immediately ahead, the world will need many trumpets to sound the clarion call. The world will need many voices to speak the words of truth and healing for which millions long. The world will need many hearts joined together in the work of the soul, and prepared to do the work of God.

Can you honestly claim that you are not aware of this?

No.

Can you honestly deny that this is why you came?

144

No.

Are you ready then, with this book, to decide and to declare your own Eternal Truth, and to announce and articulate the glory of Mine?

Must I include these last few exchanges in the book?

You don't *have* to do anything. Remember, in *our* relationship you have no obligation. Only opportunity. Is this not the opportunity for which you have waited all your life? Have you not devoted your Self to this mission—and the proper preparation for it—from the *earliest moments of youth?*

Yes.

Then do not what you are obliged to do, but what you have an opportunity to do.

As to placing all this in our book, why would you not? Think you that I want you to be a messenger in secret?

No, I suppose not.

It takes great courage to announce oneself as a man of God. You understand, the world will much more readily accept you as virtually anything else—but a man of God? An actual *messenger?* Every one of My messengers has been defiled. Far from gaining glory, they have gained nothing but heartache.

Are you willing? Does your heart *ache* to tell the truth about Me? Are you willing to endure the ridicule of your fellow human beings? Are you prepared to give *up* glory on Earth for the greater glory of the soul fully realized?

You're making this all sound suddenly pretty heavy, God.

You want I should kid you about it?

Well, we could just lighten up a little here.

Hey, I'm all for *enlightenment!* Why don't we end this chapter with a joke?

Good idea. You got one?

No, but you do. Tell the one about the little girl drawing a picture. . .

Oh, yes, that one. Okay. Well, a Mommy came into the kitchen one day to find her little girl at the table, crayons everywhere, deeply concentrating on a freehand picture she was creating. "My, what are you so busy drawing?" the Mommy asked. "It's a picture of God, Mommy," the beautiful girl replied, eyes shining. "Oh honey, that's so sweet," the Mommy said, trying to be helpful. "But you know, no one really knows what God looks like."
"Well," chirped the little girl, "if you'll just let me *finish*. . ."

That's a beautiful little joke. Do you know what's most beautiful? The little girl *never doubted* that she knew *exactly* how to draw Me!

Yes.

Now I'll tell you a story, and with that we can end this chapter.

Alright.

There once was a man who suddenly found himself spending hours each week writing a book. Day after day he would race to pad and pen—sometimes in the middle of the night—to capture each new inspiration. Finally, someone asked him what he was up to.

"Oh," he replied, "I'm writing down a very long conversation I'm having with God."

"That's very sweet," his friend indulged him, "but you know, no one really knows for sure what God would say."

"Well," the man grinned, "if you'll just *let me finish*."

9

You may think this is easy, this "be Who You Really Are" business, but it's the most challenging thing you'll ever do in your life. In fact, you may never get there. Few people do. Not in one lifetime. Not in many.

So why try? Why enter the fray? Who needs it? Why not simply play life as if it were what it apparently is anyway—a simple exercise in meaninglessness leading to nowhere in particular, a game you can't lose no matter how you play; a process that leads to the same result, ultimately, for everyone? You say there is no hell, there is no punishment, there is no way to lose, so why bother trying to win? What is the incentive, given how difficult it is to get where You say we're trying to go? Why not take our good-natured time and just relax about all this God-stuff, and "being Who You Really Are."

My, we *are* frustrated aren't we. . .

Well, I get tired of trying, trying, trying, only to have You come here and tell me how hard it's all going to be, and how only one in a million makes it anyway.

Yes, I see that you do. Let Me see if I can help. First, I would like to point out that you already *have* taken your "good-natured time" about it. Do you think this is your first attempt at this?

I have no idea.

It doesn't seem as if you've been here before?

Sometimes.

Well, you have. Many times.

How many times?

Many times.

That's supposed to encourage me?

It's supposed to inspire you.

How so?

First, it takes the worry out of it. It brings in the "can't fail" element you just talked about. It assures you that the intention is for you *not* to fail. That you'll get *as many chances as you want and need.* You can come back again and again and again. If you do get to the next step, if you evolve to the next level, it's because you *want* to, not because you *have* to.

You don't *have* to do anything! If you enjoy life at this level, if you feel this is the ultimate for you, you can have this experience over and over and over again! In fact, you *have* had it over and over again—for exactly that reason! You *love* the drama. You *love* the pain. You love the "not knowing," the mystery, the suspense! You love it all! That's why you're *here*!

Are You kidding me?

Would I kid you about a thing like that?

I don't know. I don't know what God kids about.

Not about this. This is too close to the Truth; too close to Ultimate Knowing. I never kid about "how it is." Too many people have played with your mind about that. I'm not here to get you more mixed up. I'm here to help you get things clarified.

So clarify. You're telling me I'm here because I *want* to be?

Of course. Yes.

I *chose* to be?

Yes.

And I've made that choice many times?

Many.

How many?

Here we go again. You want an exact count?

Just give me a ballpark estimate. I mean are we talking about handfuls here, or dozens?

Hundreds.

Hundreds? I've lived *hundreds of lives?*

Yes.

And this is as far as I've gotten?

This is quite some distance, actually.

Oh, it *is*, is it?

Absolutely. Why, in past lives you've actually killed people.

What's wrong with that? You said yourself that sometimes war is necessary to end evil.

We're going to have to elaborate on that, because I can see that statement being used and misused—just as you're doing now—to try to make all sorts of points, or rationalize all sorts of insanity.

By the highest standards I have observed humans devise, killing can never be justified as a means of expressing anger, releasing hostility, "righting a wrong," or punishing an offender. The statement that war is sometimes necessary to end evil stands true—for you have made it so. You have determined, in the creation of Self, that respect for all human life is, and must be, a high prime value. I am pleased with your decision, because I did not create life that it may be destroyed.

It is respect for *life* which sometimes makes war necessary, for it is through war against immediate impending evil, it is through defense against immediate threat to *another* life, that you make a statement of Who You Are in relationship to that.

You have a right under highest moral law—indeed, you have an obligation under that law—to stop aggression on the person of another, or yourself.

This does not mean that killing as a punishment is appropriate, nor as retribution, nor as a means of settling petty differences.

In your past, you have killed in personal duels over the affection of a *woman*, for heaven's sake, and called this *protecting your honor*, when it was all honor you were *losing*. It is absurd to use deadly force as an *argument solver*. Many humans are *still* using force—killing force—to solve ridiculous arguments even today.

Reaching to the height of hypocrisy, some humans even kill *in the name of God*—and that is the highest blasphemy, for it does not speak of Who You Are.

Oh, then there *is* something wrong with killing?

Let's back up. There's nothing "wrong" with *any-thing*. "Wrong" is a relative term, indicating the oppo-site of that which you call "right."

Yet, what is "right"? Can you be truly objective in these matters? Or are "right" and "wrong" simply de-scriptions overlaid on events and circumstances by you, out of your decision about them?

And what, pray tell, forms the *basis* of your decision? Your own *experience*? No. In most cases, you've chosen to accept someone *else's* decision. Someone who came before you and, presumably, knows better. Very few of your daily decisions about what is "right" and "wrong" are being made by *you*, based on *your* understanding.

This is especially true on important matters. In fact, the more important the matter, the less likely are you to listen to your own experience, and the more ready you seem to be to make someone else's ideas your own.

This explains why you've given up virtually total control over certain areas of your life, and certain questions that arise within the human experience.

These areas and questions very often include the subjects most *vital* to your soul: the nature of God; the nature of true morality; the question of ultimate reality; the issues of life and death surrounding war, medicine, abortion, euthanasia, the whole sum and substance of personal values, structures, judgments. These most of you have abrogated, assigned to others. You don't want to make your own decisions about them.

"Someone else decide! I'll go along, I'll go along!" you shout. "Someone else just tell me what's right and wrong!"

This is why, by the way, human religions are so popular. It almost doesn't matter what the belief system is, as long as it's firm, consistent, clear in its expectation of the follower, and rigid. Given those characteristics, you can find people who believe in almost anything. The strangest behavior and belief can be—has been—attrib-uted to God. It's God's way, they say. God's word.

And there are those who will *accept* that. *Gladly.*

Because, you see, *it eliminates the need to think.*

Now, let's think about killing. Can there ever be a justifiable reason for killing anything? Think about it. You'll find you need no outside authority to give you direction, no higher source to supply you with answers. If you think about it, if you look to see what you feel about it, the answers will be obvious to you, and you will act accordingly. This is called acting on your own authority.

It is when you act on the authority of others that you get yourself into trouble. Should states and nations use killing to achieve their political objectives? Should religions use killing to enforce their theological imperatives? Should societies use killing as a response to those who violate behavioral codes?

Is killing an appropriate political remedy, spiritual convincer, or societal problem solver?

Now, is killing something you can do if someone is trying to kill *you?* Would you use killing force to defend the life of a loved one? Someone you didn't even know?

Is killing a proper form of *defense* against those who would kill if they are not in some other way stopped?

Is there a difference between killing and murder?

The state would have you believe that killing to complete a purely political agenda is perfectly defensible. In fact, the state *needs* you to take its word on this in order to exist as an entity of power.

Religions would have you believe that killing to spread and maintain knowledge of, and adherence to, their particular truth is perfectly defensible. In fact, religions *require* you to take their word on this in order to exist as an entity of power.

Society would have you believe that killing to punish those who commit certain offenses (these have changed through the years) is perfectly defensible. In fact, society must have you take its word for it in order to exist as an entity of power.

Do you believe these positions are correct? Have you taken another's word for it? What does your Self have to say?

There is no "right" or "wrong" in these matters.

But by your decisions you paint a portrait of Who You Are.

Indeed, by their decisions your states and nations have already painted such pictures.

By their decisions your religions have created lasting, indelible impressions. By their decisions your societies have produced their self-portraits, too.

Are you pleased with these pictures? Are these the impressions you wish to make? Do these portraits represent Who You Are?

Be careful of these questions. They may require you to think.

Thinking is hard. Making value judgments is difficult. It places you at pure creation, because there are so many times you'll have to say, "I don't *know*. I just don't *know*." Yet still you'll have to decide. And so you'll have to *choose*. You'll have to make an arbitrary choice.

Such a choice—a decision coming from *no previous personal knowledge*--is called *pure creation*. And the individual is aware, deeply aware, that in the making of such decisions is the *Self* created.

Most of you are not interested in such important work. Most of you would rather leave that to others. And so most of you are not self-created, but creatures of habit—other-created creatures.

Then, when others have told you how you should feel, and it runs directly counter to how you *do* feel—you experience a deep inner conflict. Something deep inside you tells you that what others have told you is *not Who You Are*. Now where to go with that? What to do?

The first place you go is to your religionists—the people who put you there in the first place. You go to your priests and your rabbis and your ministers and your teachers, and they tell you to *stop listening* to your Self. The worst of them will try to *scare* you away from it; scare you away from what you intuitively *know*.

They'll tell you about the devil, about Satan, about

demons and evil spirits and hell and damnation and every frightening thing *they* can think of to get *you* to see how what you were intuitively knowing and feeling was *wrong*, and how the only place you'll find any comfort is in *their* thought, *their* idea, *their* theology, *their* definitions of right and wrong, and *their* concept of Who You Are.

The seduction here is that all you have to do to get instant approval is to *agree*. Agree and you have instant approval. Some will even sing and shout and dance and wave their arms in hallelujah!

That's hard to resist. Such approval, such rejoicing that you have seen the light; that you've been *saved!*

Approvals and demonstrations seldom accompany inner decisions. Celebrations rarely surround choices to follow personal truth. In fact, quite the contrary. Not only may others fail to celebrate, they may actually subject you to ridicule. What? You're thinking for *yourself?* You're deciding on *your own?* You're applying your own yardsticks, your own judgments, your own values? *Who do you think you are, anyway?*

And, indeed, *that is precisely the question you are answering.*

But the work must be done very much alone. Very much without reward, without approval, perhaps without even any notice.

And so you ask a very good question. Why go on? Why even start off on such a path? What is to be gained from embarking on such a journey? Where *is* the incentive? What *is* the reason?

The reason is ridiculously simple.

THERE IS NOTHING ELSE TO DO.

What do You mean?

I mean this is the only game in town. There is nothing else to do. In fact, there is nothing else you *can* do. You are going to be doing what you are doing for the rest of your life—just as you have been doing it since birth. The only question is whether you'll be doing it consciously, or unconsciously.

You see, you cannot *disembark* from the journey. You embarked before you were born. Your birth is simply a sign that the journey has begun.

So the question is not: Why start off on such a path? You have *already* started off. You did so with the first beat of your heart. The question is: Do I wish to walk this path consciously, or unconsciously? With awareness or lack of awareness? As the cause of my experience, or at the effect of it?

For most of your life you've lived at the effect of your experiences. Now, you're invited to be the cause of them. That is what is known as conscious living. That is what is called *walking in awareness*.

Now, many of you have walked quite some distance, as I've said. You have made no small progress. So you should not feel that after all these lives you've "only" come to this. Some of you are highly evolved creatures, with a very sure sense of Self. You know Who You Are and you know what you'd like to become. Furthermore, you even know the way to get from here to there.

That's a great sign. That's a sure indication.

Of what?

Of the fact that you now have very few lives left.

Is that good?

It is, now—for you. And that is so because you say it is so. Not long ago all you wanted to do was stay here. Now, all you want to do is leave. That's a very good sign.

Not long ago you killed things—bugs, plants, trees, animals, *people*—now you cannot kill a thing without knowing exactly what you're doing, and why. That's a very good sign.

Not long ago you lived life as though it had no purpose. Now you *know* it has no purpose, save the one *you give it. That's* a very good sign.

Not long ago you begged the universe to bring you Truth. Now you *tell* the universe *your* truth. And that's a *very* good sign.

Not long ago you sought to be rich and famous. Now you seek to be simply, and wonderfully, your *Self*.

And not so very long ago you *feared* Me. Now you *love* Me, enough to call Me your equal.

All of these are very, *very* good signs.

Well, gosh. . .You make me feel good.

You *should* feel good. Anybody who uses "gosh" in a sentence can't be all bad.

You really *do* have a sense of humor, don't You. . .

I *invented* humor!

Yes, You've made that point. Okay, so the reason for going on is that there's nothing else to do. This is what's happening here.

Precisely.

Then may I ask You—does it at least get any easier?

Oh, my darling friend—it is so much easier for you *now* than it was three lifetimes ago, I can't even tell you.

Yes, yes—it does get easier. The more you remember, the more you are able to experience, the more you know, so to speak. And the more you know, the more you remember. It is a circle. So yes, it gets easier, it gets better, it becomes even more joyful.

But remember, *none* of it has been exactly a drudge. I mean, you've loved *all* of it! Every last minute! Oh, it's

delicious, this thing called life! It's a scrumptious experience, no?

Well, yes, I suppose.

You _suppose?_ How much more scrumptious could
I have made it? Are you not being allowed to experience
everything? The tears, the joy, the pain, the gladness,
the exaltation, the massive depression, the win, the
lose, the draw? What more _is_ there?

A little less pain, perhaps.

Less pain without more wisdom defeats your purpose; does not allow you to experience infinite
joy—which is What I Am.
Be patient. You _are_ gaining wisdom. And your joys
are now increasingly available _without_ pain. That, too,
is a very good sign.
You are learning (remembering how) to love without
pain; to let go without pain; to create without pain; to
even cry without pain. Yes, you're even able to _have
your pain_ without pain, if you know what I mean.

I think I do. I'm enjoying even my own life dramas more. I
can stand back and see them for what they are. Even laugh.

Exactly. And you don't call this growth?

I suppose I do.

And so then, keep on growing, My son. Keep on
becoming. And keep on deciding what you want to
become in the next highest version of your Self. Keep
on working toward that. Keep on! Keep on! This is God
Work we're up to, you and I. So keep on!

10

I love You, You know that?

I know you do. And I love you.

11

I'd like to get back to my list of questions. There's so much more detail I want to go into on every one of these. We could do a whole book on relationships alone, and I know that. But then I'd never get to my other questions.

There'll be other times, other places. Even other books. I'm with you. Let's move on. We'll come back to it here if we have time.

Okay. My next question, then: Why can't I ever seem to attract enough money in my life? Am I destined to be forever scrimping and scraping? What is blocking me from realizing my full potential regarding money?

The condition is manifested not just by you, but by a great many people.

Everyone tells me it's a problem of self-worth; a lack of self-worth. I've had a dozen New Age teachers tell me that lack of anything is always traceable to lack of self-worth.

That is a convenient simplification. In this case your teachers are wrong. You do not suffer from a lack of self-worth. Indeed, your greatest challenge all your life has been to control your ego. Some have said it's been a case of too *much* self-worth!

Well, here I am, embarrassed and chagrined again, but You are right.

You keep saying you're embarrassed and chagrined

every time I simply tell the truth about you. *Embarrassment is the response of a person who still has an ego investment in how others see him. Invite yourself to move past that. Try a new response. Try laughter.*

Okay.

Self-worth is not your problem. You are blessed with an abundance of it. Most people are. You all think very highly of yourself, as rightly you should. So self-worth, for the great mass of the people, is not the problem.

What is?

The problem is lack of understanding of the principles of abundance together, usually, with a massive misjudgment about what is "good" and what is "evil."
Let Me give you an example.

Please do.

You carry a thought around that money is bad. You also carry a thought around that God is good. Bless you! Therefore, in your thought system, God and money do not mix.

Well, in a sense, I guess, that's true. That *is* how I think.

This makes things interesting, because this then makes it difficult for you to take money for any good thing.
I mean, if a thing is judged very "good" by you, you value it *less* in terms of money. So the "better" something is (i.e., the more worthwhile), the less *money* it's worth.
You are not alone in this. Your whole society believes this. So your teachers make a pittance and your stripteasers, a fortune. Your leaders make so little compared to sports figures that they feel they have to steal

to make up the difference. Your priests and your rabbis live on bread and water while you *throw* coins at entertainers.

Think about it. Everything on which you place a high *intrinsic* value, you insist must come cheaply. The lonely research scientist seeking a cure for AIDS goes begging for money, while the woman who writes a book on a hundred new ways to have sex and creates tapes and weekend seminars to go with it. . .makes a fortune.

This having-it-all-backwards is a propensity with you, and it stems from wrong thought.

The wrong thought is your idea about money. You love it, and yet you say it is the root of all evil. You adore it, and yet you call it "filthy lucre." You say that a person is "filthy rich." And if a person *does* become wealthy doing "good" things, you immediately become suspect. You make that "wrong."

So, a doctor had better not make *too* much money, or had better learn to be discreet about it. And a *minister*—whoa! She'd *really* better not make lots of money (assuming you'll even let a "she" *be* a minister), or there'll surely be trouble.

You see, in *your* mind, a person who chooses the highest calling should get the lowest pay. . .

Hmmm.

Yes, "hmmm" is right. You *should* think about that. Because it is such wrong thought.

I thought there was no such thing as wrong or right.

There isn't. There is only what serves you, and what does not. The terms "right" and "wrong" are relative terms, and I use them that way when I use them at all. In this case, relative to what serves you—relative to what you *say you want*—your money thoughts are wrong thoughts.

....

Remember, thoughts are creative. So if you think money is bad, yet think yourself good. . .well, you can see the conflict.

Now you, in particular, My son, act out this race consciousness in a very big way. For most people the conflict is not nearly so enormous as for you. Most people do what they hate for a living, so they don't mind taking money for it. "Bad" for the "bad," so to speak. But you love what you do with the days and times of your life. You adore the activities with which you cram them.

For you, therefore, to receive large amounts of money for what you do would be, in your thought system, taking "bad" for the "good" and that is unacceptable to you. You'd rather starve than take "filthy lucre" for pure service. . .as if somehow the service loses its purity if you take money for it.

So here we have this real ambivalence about money. Part of you rejects it, and part of you resents not having it. Now, the universe doesn't know what to do about that, because the universe has received two different thoughts from you. So your life with regard to money is going to go in fits and starts, because you keep going in fits and starts about money.

You don't have a clear focus; you're not really sure what's true for you. And the universe is just a big Xerox machine. It simply produces multiple copies of your thoughts.

Now there's only one way to change all that. You have to change your *thought* about it.

How can I change the way I *think*? The way I think about something is the way I think about something. My thoughts, my attitudes, my ideas were not created in a minute. I have to guess they are the result of years of experience, a lifetime of encounters. You are right about the way I think about money, but how do I change that?

This could be the most interesting question in the book. The usual method of creation for most human beings is a three-step process involving thought, word, and deed, or action.

First comes thought; the formative idea; the initial concept. Then comes the word. Most thoughts ultimately form themselves into words, which are often then written or spoken. This gives added energy to the thought, pushing it out into the world, where it can be noticed by others.

Finally, in some cases words are put into action, and you have what you call a result; a physical world manifestation of what all started with a thought.

Everything around you in your man-made world came into being in this way—or some variation of it. All three creation centers were used.

But now comes the question: how to change a Sponsoring Thought?

Yes, that is a very good question. And a very important one. For if humans do not change some of their Sponsoring Thoughts, humankind could doom itself to extinction.

The most rapid way to change a root thought, or sponsoring idea, is to *reverse the thought-word-deed process*.

Explain that.

Do the deed that you want to have the new thought about. Then say the words that you want to have your new thought about. Do this often enough and you'll train the mind to *think a new way*.

Train the mind? Isn't that like mind control? Isn't that just mental manipulation?

Do you have any idea how your mind came up with the thoughts it *now* has? Do you not know that your world has manipulated your mind to think as you do? *Wouldn't it be better for* you *to manipulate your mind than for the world to?*

Would you not be better off to think the thoughts *you* want to think, than those of others? Are you not better armed with creative thoughts than with reactive thoughts?

Yet your mind is filled with reactive thought—thought that springs from the experience of others. Very few of your thoughts spring from self-produced data, much less self-produced preferences.

Your own root thought about money is a prime example. Your thought about money (it is bad) runs directly counter to your experience (it's great to have money!). So you have to run around and lie to yourself about your experience in order to justify your root thought.

You are so *rooted* in this thought, it never occurs to you that your *idea* about money *may be inaccurate.*

So now what we are up to is coming up with some self-produced data. And *that* is how we change a root thought, and cause it to be *your* root thought, not another's.

You have one more root thought about money, by the way, which I've yet to mention.

What's that?

That there's not enough. In fact you have this root thought about just about everything. There's not enough money, there's not enough time, there's not enough love, there's not enough food, water, compassion in the world. . .Whatever there is that's good, there's just *not enough.*

This race consciousness of "not-enough-ness" creates and recreates the world as you see it.

Okay, so I have two root thoughts—Sponsoring Thoughts—to change about money.

Oh, at least two. Probably many more. Let's see. money is bad. . .money is scarce. . .money may not be received for doing God's work (that's a big one with you). . .money is never given freely. . .money doesn't grow on trees (when, in fact, it does). . .money corrupts.

I see I've got a lot of work to do.

Yes, you do, if you're not happy with your present money situation. On the other hand, it's important to understand that you're unhappy with your present money situation *because* you're unhappy with your present money situation.

Sometimes You're hard to follow.

Sometimes you're hard to lead.

Say, listen, You're the God here. Why don't You make it easy to understand?

I *have* made it easy to understand.

Then why don't You just *cause* me to understand, if that's what You truly want?

I truly want what you truly want—nothing different and nothing more. Don't you see that is My greatest gift to you? If I wanted for you something other than what you want for you, and then went so far as to *cause you to have it*, where is your free choice? How can you be a creative being if I am dictating what you shall be, do, and have? *My joy is in your freedom, not your compliance.*

Okay, what did You mean, I'm unhappy with my money situation because I'm unhappy with my money situation?

You are what you think you are. It's a vicious circle when the thought is a negative one. You've got to find a way to break out of the circle.

So much of your present experience is based on your previous thought. Thought leads to experience, which leads to thought, which leads to experience. This can produce constant joy when the Sponsoring Thought is joyous. It can, and does, produce continual hell when the Sponsoring Thought is hellatious.

The trick is to change Sponsoring Thought. I was about to illustrate how to do that.

Go.

Thank you.

The first thing to do is reverse the thought-word-deed paradigm. Do you remember the old adage, "Think before you act"?

Yes.

Well, forget it. If you want to change a root thought, you have to act *before you think.*

Example: you're walking down the street and come across an old lady begging for quarters. You realize she's a bag lady and is living day-to-day. You instantly know that as little money as you have, you surely have enough to share with her. Your first impulse is to give her some change. There's even a part of you that's ready to reach in your pocket for a little folding money—a one, or even a five. What the heck, make it a grand moment for her. Light her up.

Then, thought comes in. What, are you crazy? We've only got seven dollars to get *us* through the day! You want to give her a five? So you start fumbling around for that one.

Thought again: Hey, hey, c'mon. You don't have that many of these that you can just *give them away!* Give her

__ Conversations with God _____

some coins, for heaven's sake, and let's get out of here.

Quickly you reach into the other pocket to try to come up with some quarters. Your fingers feel only nickels and dimes. You're embarrassed. Here you are, fully clothed, fully fed, and you're going to nickel-and-dime this poor woman who has nothing.

You try in vain to find a quarter or two. Oh, there's one, deep in the fold of your pocket. But by now you've walked past her, smiling wanly, and it's too late to go back. She gets nothing. You get nothing, either. Instead of the joy of knowing your abundance and sharing, you now feel as poor as the woman.

Why didn't you *just give her the paper money!* It was your first impulse, but your thought got in the way.

Next time, decide to act before you think. Give the money. Go ahead! You've got it, and there's more where that came from. That's the only thought which separates you from the bag lady. You're clear there's more where that came from, and she doesn't know that.

When you want to change a root thought, act in accordance with the new idea you have. But you must act quickly, or your mind will kill the idea before you know it. I mean that literally. The idea, the new truth, will be dead in you *before you've had a chance to know it.*

So act quickly when the opportunity arises, and, if you do this often enough, your mind will soon *get the idea.* It will be your new thought.

Oh, I just got something! Is that what's meant by the New Thought Movement?

If not, it should be. New thought is your only chance. It's your only real opportunity to evolve, to grow, to truly become Who You Really Are.

Your mind is right now filled with old thoughts. Not only old thoughts, but mostly someone else's old thoughts. It's important now, it's time now, to *change your mind* about some things. This is what evolution is all about.

12

Why can't I do what I really want to do with my life and still make a living?

What? You mean you actually want to have *fun* in your life, and still earn your keep? Brother, are *you* dreaming!

What?—

Only kidding—just doing a little mind reading, that's all. You see, that's been *your* thought about it.

It's been my experience.

Yes. Well, we've been all through this now a number of times. The people who make a living doing what they love are the people who insist on doing so. They don't give up. They never give in. They dare life *not* to let them do what they love.

But there's another element that must be brought up, because this is the missing element in most people's understanding when it comes to life work.

What's that?

There's a difference between being and doing, and most people have placed their emphasis on the latter.

Shouldn't they?

There's no "should" or "should not" involved. There's only what you choose, and how you can have it. If you choose peace and joy and love, you won't get much of it through what you're doing. If you choose happiness and contentment, you'll find little of that on the path of doingness. If you choose reunion with God, supreme knowing, deep understanding, endless compassion, total awareness, absolute fulfillment, you won't achieve much of that out of what you're doing.

In other words, if you choose *evolution*—the evolution of your soul—you won't produce that by the worldly activities of your body.

Doing is a function of the body. *Being* is a function of the soul. The body is always doing *something*. Every minute of every day it's up to *something*. It never stops, it never rests, it's constantly *doing* something.

It's either doing what it's doing at the behest of the soul—or in spite of the soul. The quality of your life hangs in the balance.

The soul is forever *being*. It is being what it is being, regardless of what the body is doing, not *because* of what it's doing.

If you think your life is about doingness, you do not understand what you are about.

Your soul doesn't care *what* you do for a living—and when your life is over, neither will you. Your soul cares only about what you're *being* while you're doing *whatever* you're doing.

It is a state of beingness the soul is after, not a state of doingness.

What is the soul seeking to be?

Me.

You.

Yes, Me. Your soul *is* Me, and it knows it. What it is doing, is trying to *experience that*. And what it is remem-

bering is that the best way to have this experience is by
not doing anything. There is nothing to do but to be.

Be what?

Whatever you want to be. Happy. Sad. Weak.
Strong. Joyful. Vengeful. Insightful. Blind. Good. Bad.
Male. Female. You name it.
I mean that literally. _You name it._

This is all very profound, but what does it have to do with
my career? I'm trying to find a way to stay alive, to survive, to
support myself and my family, doing what I like to do.

Try being what you like to be.

What do you mean?

Some people make lots of money doing what they
do, others can't make a go of it—and they're _doing the
same thing._ What makes the difference?

Some people have more skill than others.

That's the first cut. But now we get to the second cut.
Now we're down to two people with relatively equal
skills. Both graduated from college, both were at the top
of their class, both understand the nature of what they're
doing, both know how to use their tools with great
facility—yet one still does better than the other; one
flourishes while the other struggles. What's that about?

Location.

Location?

Somebody once told me there are only three things to consider
when starting a new business—location, location, and location.

In other words, not "What are you going to do?" but "Where are you going to be?"

Exactly.

That sounds like the answer to my question as well. The soul is concerned only with where you are going to be.

Are you going to be in a place called fear, or in a place called love? Where *are* you—and where are you coming *from*—as you encounter life?

Now, in the example of the two equally qualified workers, one is successful and the other is not, not because of anything either is doing, but because of what both are being.

One person is being open, friendly, caring, helpful, considerate, cheerful, confident, even joyful in her work, while the other is being closed, distant, uncaring, inconsiderate, grumpy, even resentful of what she is doing.

Now suppose you were to select even loftier states of beingness? Suppose you were to select goodness, mercy, compassion, understanding, forgiveness, love? What if you were to select Godliness? What *then* would be your experience?

I tell you this:

Beingness attracts beingness, and produces experience.

You are not on this planet to produce anything with your body. You are on this planet to produce something with your soul. Your body is simply and merely the tool of your soul. Your mind is the power that makes the body go. So what you have here is a power tool, used in the creation of the soul's desire.

What *is* the soul's desire?

Indeed, what is it?

I don't know. I'm asking You.

I don't know. I'm asking you.

This could go on forever.

It has.

Wait a minute! A moment ago You said the soul is seeking to be _You_.

So it is.

Then _that_ is the soul's desire.

In the broadest sense, yes. But this Me it is seeking to be is very complex, very multi-dimensional, multi-sensual, multi-faceted. There are a million aspects to Me. A billion. A trillion. You see? There is the profane and the profound, the lesser and the larger, the hollow and the holy, the ghastly and the Godly. You see?

Yes, yes, I see. . .the up and the down, the left and the right, the here and the there, the before and the after, the good and the bad. . .

Precisely. I _am_ the Alpha and the Omega. That was not just a pretty saying, or a nifty concept. That was Truth expressed.

So, in seeking to be Me, the soul has a grand job ahead of it; an enormous menu of _beingness_ from which to choose. And that is what it is doing in this moment now.

Choosing states of being.

Yes—and then producing the right and perfect _con-ditions_ within which to create the experience of that. It

173

is therefore true that nothing happens to you or through you that is not for your own highest good.

You mean my soul is creating all of my experience, including not only the things I am doing, but the things that are happening to me?

Let us say that the soul leads you to the right and perfect *opportunities* for you to experience exactly what you had planned to experience. What you actually experience is up to you. It could be what you planned to experience, or it could be something else, depending upon what you choose.

Why would I choose something I don't wish to experience?

I don't know. Why would you?

Do You mean that sometimes the soul wishes one thing, a..d the body or the mind wishes another?

What do you think?

But how can the body, or the mind, overrule the soul? Doesn't the soul always get what it wants?

The spirit of you seeks, in the largest sense, that grand moment when you have conscious awareness of its wishes, and join in joyful oneness with them. But the spirit will never, ever, force its desire on the present, conscious, physical part of you.

The Father will not force His will upon the Son. It is a violation of His very nature to do so, and thus, quite literally, impossible.

The Son will not force His will upon the Holy Spirit. It is against His very nature to do so, and thus, quite literally, impossible.

The Holy Spirit will not force His will upon your soul.

It is outside of the nature of the spirit to do so, and thus, quite literally, impossible.

Here is where the impossibilities end. The mind very often *does* seek to exert its will on the body—and does so. Similarly, the body seeks often to control the mind—and frequently succeeds.

Yet the body and the mind together do not have to do anything to control the soul—for the soul is completely without need (unlike the body and the mind, which are shackled with it), and so allows the body and the mind to have their way all the time.

Indeed, the soul would have it no other way—for if the entity which is you is to create, and thus know, who it really is, it must be through an act of conscious volition, not an act of unconscious obedience.

Obedience is not creation, and thus can never produce salvation.

Obedience is a response, while creation is pure choice, undictated, unrequired.

Pure choice produces salvation through the pure creation of highest idea in this moment now.

The function of the soul is to *indicate* its desire, not *impose* it.

The function of the mind is to *choose* from its alternatives.

The function of the body is to *act out* that choice.

When body, mind, and soul create together, in harmony and in unity, God is made flesh.

Then does the soul know itself in its own experience.

Then do the heavens rejoice.

Right now, in this moment, your soul has again created opportunity for you to be, do, and have what it takes to know Who You Really Are.

Your soul has *brought* you to the words you are reading right now—as it has brought you to words of wisdom and truth before.

What will you do now? What will you choose to be?

Your soul waits, and watches with interest, as it has many times before.

Do I understand You to say that it is out of the state of beingness I select that my worldly success (I am still trying to talk about my career here) will be determined?

I am not concerned about your worldly success, only you are.

It is true that when you achieve certain states of being over a long period of time, success in what you are doing in the world is very difficult to avoid. Yet you are not to worry about "making a living." *True Masters are those who have chosen to make a life, rather than a living.*

From certain states of being will spring a life so rich, so full, so magnificent, and so rewarding that worldly goods and worldly success will be of no concern to you.

Life's irony is that as soon as worldly goods and worldly success are of no concern to you, the way is open for them to flow to you.

Remember, you cannot have what you want, but you may experience whatever you have.

I cannot have what I want?

No.

You said this before, very early in our dialogue. Still, I don't understand. I thought you've been telling me I could have *whatever* I want. "As you think, as you believe, so shall it be done unto you," and all that.

The two statements are not inconsistent with each other.

They aren't? They sure feel inconsistent to me.

That is because you lack understanding.

Well, I admit that. That's why I'm talking with You.

I will then explain. You cannot have *anything* you want. The very act of wanting something pushes it away from you, as I said earlier, in Chapter One.

Well, You may have said it earlier, but You're losing me—fast.

Fight to keep up. I'll go over it again in greater detail. Try to stay with it. Let's go back to a point you do understand: *thought is creative*. Okay?

Okay.

Word is creative. Got it?

Got it.

Action is creative. Thought, word, and deed are the three levels of creation. Still with Me?

Right there.

Good. Now let's take "worldly success" as our subject for the moment, since that's what you've been talking about, asking about.

Terrific.

Now, do you have a thought, "I want worldly success"?

Sometimes, yes.

And do you also sometimes have the thought, "I want more money"?

Yes.

You can therefore neither have worldly success *nor*
more money.

Why *not?*

Because the universe has no choice but to bring you
the direct manifestation of your thought about it.
Your thought is, "I want worldly success." You understand, the creative power is like a genie in a bottle.
Your words are its command. You understand?

Then why don't I have more success?

I said, your words are its command. Now your *words*
were, "I want success." And the universe says, "Okay,
you do."

I'm still not sure I follow.

Think of it this way. The word "I" is the key that starts
the engine of creation. The words "I am" are extremely
powerful. They are statements to the universe. Commands.
Now, whatever follows the word "I" (which calls forth
the Great I Am) tends to manifest in physical reality.
Therefore "I" + "want success" produces you *wanting
success.* "I" + "want money" must produce you *wanting
money.* It can produce no other thing, because thoughts,
words are creative. Actions are, too. And if you *act* in a
way which says that you want success and money, then
your thoughts, words, *and* actions are in accord, and you
are *sure* to have the experience of this wantingness.
You see?

Yes! My God—does it really work that way?

Of course! You are a *very powerful creator.* Now
granted, if you had a thought, or made a statement, just

once—as in anger, for instance, or frustration, it's not very likely that you'll convert those thoughts or words into reality. So you don't have to worry about "Drop dead!" or "Go to hell," or all the other less-than-nice things you sometimes think or say.

Thank God.

You're welcome. But, if you repeat a thought, or say a word, over and over again—not once, not twice, but dozens, hundreds, thousands of times—do you have any idea of the creative power of that?
A thought or a word expressed and expressed and expressed becomes just that—expressed. *That is, pushed out. It becomes outwardly realized. It becomes your physical reality.*

Good grief.

That's exactly what it produces very often—*good grief.* You love the grief, you love the drama. That is, until you don't anymore. There comes a certain point in your evolution when you cease to love the drama, cease to love the "story" as you've been living it. That's when you decide—actively choose—to change it. Only most don't know how. You now do. To change your reality, simply *stop thinking like that.*
In this case, instead of thinking "I want success," think "I have success."

That feels like a lie to me. I'd be kidding myself if I said that. My mind would shout, "The hell you say!"

Then think a thought you *can* accept. "My success is coming to me now," or "all things lead to my success."

So this is the trick behind the New Age practice of affirmations.

Affirmations do not work if they are merely state-
ments of what you want to be true. Affirmations work
only when they are statements of something you already
know to be true.

The best so-called affirmation is a statement of
gratitude and appreciation. "Thank you, God, for bringing me success in my life." Now, *that* idea, thought,
spoken, and acted upon, produces wonderful results—when it comes from true knowing; not from an
attempt to *produce* results, but from an awareness that
results have *already* been produced.

Jesus had such clarity. Before every miracle, He
thanked Me in advance for its deliverance. It never
occurred to Him not to be grateful, because it never
occurred to Him that what He declared would not
happen. The thought *never entered His mind*.

So *sure* was He of Who He Was and of His relationship to Me that His every thought, word, and deed
reflected his awareness—just as *your* thoughts, words,
and deeds reflect yours. . .

If, now, there is something you choose to experience
in your life, do not "want" it—choose it.

Do you choose success in worldly terms? Do you
choose more money? *Good.* Then *choose* it. Really.
Fully. Not half-heartedly.

Yet at your stage of development do not be surprised
if "worldly success" no longer concerns you.

What is that supposed to mean?

There comes a time in the evolution of every soul
when the chief concern is no longer the survival of the
physical body, but the growth of the spirit; no longer
the attainment of worldly success, but the realization of
Self.

In a sense, this is a very dangerous time, particularly at the outset, because the entity housed in the
body now knows it is just that: a being in a body—not
a body-being.

At this stage, before the growing entity matures in this point of view, there is often a sense of no longer caring about affairs of the body in any way. The soul is so excited about being "discovered" at last!

The mind abandons the body, and all matters of the body. Everything is ignored. Relationships are set aside. Families are disappeared. Jobs are made secondary. Bills go unpaid. The body itself is not even fed for long periods. The entire focus and attention of the entity are now on the soul, and matters of the soul.

This can lead to a major personal crisis in the day-to-day life of the being, although the mind perceives no trauma. It is hanging out in bliss. Other people say you have lost your mind—and in a sense you may have.

Discovery of the truth that life has nothing to do with the body can create an imbalance the *other* way. Whereas at first the entity acted as if the body were all there is, now it acts as if the body matters not at all. This, of course, is not true—as the entity soon (and sometimes painfully) remembers.

You are a tri-part being, made of body, mind, and spirit. You will *always* be a tri-part being, not just while you are living on the Earth.

There are those who hypothesize that upon death the body and the mind are dropped. The body and the mind are *not* dropped. The body changes form, leaving its most dense part behind, but retaining always its outer shell. The mind (not to be confused with the brain) goes with you, too, joining with the spirit and the body as the one energy mass of three dimensions, or facets.

Should you choose to return to this experiencing opportunity that you call life on Earth, your divine self will once again separate its true dimensions into what you call body, mind, and spirit. In truth you are all one energy, yet with three distinct characteristics.

As you undertake to inhabit a new physical body here on Earth, your ethereal body (as some of you have termed it) lowers its vibrations—slows itself from a vibration so rapid that it cannot even be seen, to a speed that produces mass and matter. This actual matter is the creation of pure thought—the work of your mind, the higher mind aspect of your three-part being.

This matter is a coagulation of a million billion trillion different energy units into one enormous mass—controllable by the mind. . .you really are a master mind!

As these tiny energy units have expended their energy, they are discarded by the body, while the mind creates new ones. This the mind creates out of its continuing thought about Who You Are! The ethereal body "catches" the thought, so to speak, and lowers the vibration of more energy units (in a sense "crystallizes" them), and they become matter—the new matter of you. In this way, every cell of your body changes every several years. You are—quite literally—*not the same person* you were a few years ago.

If you think thoughts of illness or disease (or continuing anger, hatred, and negativity), your body will translate these thoughts into physical form. People will see this negative, sick form and they will say, "What's the matter?" They will not know how accurate their question is.

The soul watches this whole drama play out, year after year, month after month, day after day, moment after moment, and always holds the Truth about you. It *never* forgets the blueprint; the original plan; the first idea; the creative thought. Its job is to remind you—that is, to literally *re-mind* you—so that you may remember once again Who You Are—and then choose Who You now Wish to Be.

In this way the cycle of creation and experience, imaging and fulfilling, knowing and growing into the unknown, continues, both now and even forever more.

Whew!

Yes, exactly. Oh, and there's much more to explain. So much more. But never, ever in one book—nor probably even in one lifetime. Yet you have begun, and that is good. Just remember this. It is as your grand teacher William Shakespeare said: "There are more things in Heaven and Earth, Horatio, than are dreamt of in your philosophy."

May I ask you some questions about this? Like, when you say the mind goes with me after death, does that mean my "personality" goes with me? Will I know in the afterlife who I was?

Yes. . .and who you have *ever* been. It will *all* be opened onto you—because then it will profit you to know. Now, in this moment, it will not.

And, with regard to this life, will there be an "accounting"—a review—a tally taking?

There is no judgment in what you call the afterlife. You will not even be allowed to judge yourself (for you would surely give yourself a low score, given how judgmental and unforgiving you are with yourself in *this* life).
No, there is no accounting, no one giving "thumbs-up" or "thumbs-down." *Only humans are judgmental, and because you are, you assume that I must be. Yet I am not—and that is a great truth you cannot accept.*
Nonetheless, while there will be no judgment in the afterlife, there will be opportunity to look again at all you have thought, said, and done here, and to decide if that is what you would choose again, based on Who You say You Are, and Who You Want to Be.

There is an Eastern mystical teaching surrounding a doctrine called Kama Loca—according to this teaching, at the time of our death each person is given the opportunity to relive every thought ever entertained, every word ever spoken, every action ever taken, not from our standpoint, but from the standpoint of every other person affected. In other words, we've *already* experienced what *we* felt thinking, saying, and doing what we did—now we're given the experience of feeling what the *other* person felt in each of these moments—and it is by *this* measure that we'll decide whether we'll think, say, or do those things again. Any comment?

What occurs in your life after this is far too extraordinary to describe here in terms you could comprehend—because the experience is other-dimensional and literally defies description using tools as severely limited as words. It is enough to say that you will have the opportunity to review again this, your present life, without pain or fear or judgment, for the purpose of deciding how you feel about your experience here, and where you want to go from there.

Many of you will decide to come back here; to return to this world of density and relativity for another chance to experience out the decisions and choices you make about your Self at this level.

Others of you—a select few—will return with a different mission. You will return to density and matter for the soul purpose of bringing others *out* of density and matter. Always there are on the Earth those among you who have made such a choice. You can tell them apart at once. Their work is finished. They have returned to Earth simply and merely to help others. This is their joy. This is their exaltation. They seek naught but to be of service.

You cannot miss these people. They are everywhere. There are more of them than you think. Chances are you know one, or know of one.

Am I one?

No. If you have to ask, you know you are not one. One such as this asks questions of no one. There is nothing to ask.

You, My son, in this lifetime are a messenger. A harbinger. A bringer of news; a seeker and frequently a speaker of Truth. That is enough for one lifetime. Be happy.

Oh, I *am*. But I can always hope for more!

Yes! And you will! Always you will hope for more. It is in your nature. It is divine nature to seek always to be more.

So seek, yes, by all means *seek*.

Now I want to answer definitively the question with which you started this segment of our ongoing conversation.

Go ahead and *do* what you really love to do! Do nothing else! You have so little time. How can you think of wasting a moment doing something for a *living* you don't like to do? What kind of a living is *that*? That is not a living, that is a *dying*!

If you say, "But, but. . .I have others who depend on me. . .little mouths to feed. . .a spouse who is looking to me. . ." I will answer: If you insist that your life is about what your body is doing, you do not understand why you came here. At least do something that pleases you—that speaks of Who You Are.

Then at least you can stay out of resentment and anger toward those you imagine are keeping you from your joy.

What your body is doing is not to be discounted. It is important. But not in the way that you think. The actions of the body were meant to be reflections of a state of being, not attempts to attain a state of being.

In the true order of things one does not *do* something in order to *be* happy—one *is* happy and, hence, *does* something. One does not *do* some things in order to *be* compassionate, one *is* compassionate and, hence, acts in a certain way. The soul's decision precedes the body's action in a highly conscious person. Only an unconscious person attempts to produce a state of the soul through something the body is doing.

This is what is meant by the statement, "Your life is not about what your body is doing." Yet it _is_ true that what your body is doing is a reflection of what your life is about.

It is another divine dichotomy.

Yet, know this if you understand nothing else:

You have a _right_ to your joy; children or no children; spouse or no spouse. Seek it! Find it! And you will have a joyful family, no matter how much money you make or don't make. And if they aren't joyful, and they get up and leave you, then release them with love to seek _their_ joy.

If, on the other hand, you have evolved to the point where things of the body are not of concern to you, then you are even more free to seek your joy—on Earth as it is in heaven. God says it's _okay to be happy_—yes, even happy in your _work_.

Your life work is a statement of Who You Are. If it is not, then why are you doing it?

Do you imagine that you _have_ to?

You don't have to do anything.

If "man who supports his family, at all costs, even his own happiness" is Who You Are, then _love_ your work, because it is _facilitating_ your creation of a _living statement of Self_.

If "woman who works at job she hates in order to meet responsibilities as she sees them" is Who You Are, then love, love, _love_ your job, for it totally supports your Self image, your Self concept.

Everyone can love everything the moment they understand what they are doing, and why.

No one does anything he doesn't want to do.

13

How can I solve some of the health problems I face? I have been the victim of enough chronic problems to last three lifetimes. Why am I having them all now—in *this* lifetime?

First, let's get one thing straight. You love them. Most of them, anyway. You've used them admirably to feel sorry for yourself and to get attention for yourself.

On the few occasions when you haven't loved them, it's only because they've gone too far. Farther than you thought they ever would when you created them.

Now let's understand what you probably already know: all illness is self-created. Even conventional medical doctors are now seeing how people *make themselves sick*.

Most people do so quite unconsciously. (They don't even know what they're doing.) So when they get sick, they don't know what hit them. It feels as though something has *befallen* them, rather than that they did something to themselves.

This occurs because most people move through life—not simply health issues and consequences—unconsciously.

People smoke and wonder why they get cancer.

People ingest animals and fat and wonder why they get blocked arteries.

People stay angry all their lives and wonder why they get heart attacks.

People compete with other people—mercilessly and under incredible stress—and wonder why they have strokes.

The not-so-obvious truth is that most people *worry*

themselves to death.

Worry is just about the worst form of mental activity there is—next to hate, which is deeply self destructive. Worry is pointless. It is wasted mental energy. It also creates bio-chemical reactions which harm the body, producing everything from indigestion to coronary arrest, and a multitude of things in between.

Health will improve almost at once when *worrying* ends.

Worry is the activity of a mind which does not understand its connection with Me.

Hatred is the most severely damaging mental condition. It poisons the body, and its effects are virtually irreversible.

Fear is the opposite of everything you are, and so has an effect of opposition to your mental and physical health. *Fear is worry magnified.*

Worry, hate, fear—together with their offshoots: anxiety, bitterness, impatience, avarice, unkindness, judgmentalness, and condemnation—all attack the body at the cellular level. It is impossible to have a healthy body under these conditions.

Similarly—although to a somewhat lesser degree—conceit, self-indulgence, and greed lead to physical illness, or lack of well-*being*.

All illness is created first in the mind.

How can that be? What of conditions contracted from another? Colds—or, for that matter, AIDS?

Nothing occurs in your life—nothing—which is not first a thought. Thoughts are like magnets, drawing effects to you. The thought may not always be obvious, and thus clearly causative, as in, "I'm going to contract a terrible disease." The thought may be (and usually is) far more subtle than that. ("I am not worthy to live.") ("My life is always a mess.") ("I am a loser.") ("God is going to punish me.") ("I am sick and tired of my life!")

Thoughts are a very subtle, yet extremely powerful, form of energy. Words are less subtle, more dense. Actions are the most dense of all. Action is energy in heavy physical form, in heavy motion. When you think, say, *and* act out a negative concept such as "I am a loser," you place tremendous creative energy into motion. Small wonder you come down with a cold. That would be the least of it.

It is very difficult to reverse the effects of negative thinking once they have taken physical form. Not impossible—but very difficult. It takes an act of extreme faith. It requires an extraordinary belief in the positive force of the universe—whether you call that God, Goddess, the Unmoved Mover, Prime Force, First Cause, or whatever.

Healers have just such faith. It is a faith that crosses over into Absolute Knowing. They *know* that you are meant to be whole, complete, and perfect in *this moment now*. This knowingness is also a thought—and a very powerful one. It has the power to move mountains—to say nothing of molecules in your body. That is why healers can heal, often even at a distance.

Thought knows no distance. Thought travels around the world and traverses the universe faster than you can say the word.

"Say but the word and my servant shall be healed." And it was so, in that selfsame hour, even before his sentence was finished. Such was the faith of the centurion.

Yet *you* are all mental lepers. Your mind is eaten away with negative thoughts. Some of these are thrust upon you. Many of these you actually make up—conjure up—yourselves, and then harbor and entertain for hours, days, weeks, months—even years.

. . .and you wonder why you are sick.

You can "solve some of the health problems," as you put it, by solving the problems in your thinking. Yes, you can heal some of the conditions you have already acquired (given yourself), as well as prevent major new problems from developing. And you can do this all by changing your thinking.

Also—and I hate to suggest this because it sounds so mundane coming, as it were, from God, but—for God's sake, *take better care of yourself.*

You take rotten care of your body, paying it little attention at all until you suspect something's going wrong with it. You do virtually nothing in the way of preventive maintenance. You take better care of your *car* than you do of your body—and that's not saying much.

Not only do you fail to prevent breakdowns with regular check-ups, once-a-year physicals, and use of the therapies and medicines you've been given (why do you go to the doctor, get her help, then not use the remedies she suggests? Can you answer Me that one?)—you also mistreat your body terribly between these visits about which you do nothing!

You do not exercise it, so it grows *flabby* and, worse yet, weak from non-use.

You do not nourish it properly, thereby weakening it further.

Then you fill it with toxins and poisons and the most absurd substances posing as food. And still it runs for you, this marvelous engine; still it chugs along, bravely pushing on in the face of this on-slaught.

It's horrible. The conditions under which you ask your body to survive are horrible. But you will do little or nothing about them. You will read this, nod your head in regretful agreement, and go right back to the mistreatment. And do you know why?

I'm afraid to ask.

Because you have *no will to live.*

That seems a harsh indictment.

It's not meant to be harsh, nor is it meant as an indictment. "Harsh" is a relative term; a judgment you have laid on the words. "Indictment" connotes guilt, and "guilt" connotes wrongdoing. There is no wrongdoing involved here, hence no guilt and no indictment.

I have made a simple statement of truth. Like all statements of truth, it has the quality of waking you up. Some people don't like to be awakened. Most do not. Most would rather sleep.

The world is in the condition that it's in because the world is full of sleepwalkers.

With regard to my statement, what about it seems untrue? You *have* no will to live. At least you have had none until now.

If you tell me you've had an "instant conversion," I will reassess my prediction of what you will now do. I acknowledge that my prediction is based on past experience.

. . .it was also meant to wake you up. Sometimes, when a person is really deeply asleep, you have to shake him a little.

I have seen in the past that you have had little will to live. Now you may deny that, but in this case your actions speak louder than your words.

If you ever lit a cigarette in your life—much less smoked a pack a day for 20 years as you have—you have very little will to live. You don't care *what* you do to your body.

But I *stopped* smoking over 10 years ago!

Only after 20 years of grueling physical punishment.
And if you've ever taken alcohol into your body, you have very little will to live.

I drink very moderately.

The body was not meant to intake alcohol. It impairs the mind.

But *Jesus* took alcohol! He went to the wedding and turned water into wine!

So who said Jesus was perfect?

Oh, for God's sake.

Say, are you becoming annoyed with Me?

Well, far be it from me to become *annoyed with God*. I mean, that would be a bit presumptuous, wouldn't it? But I do think we can carry all this a bit too far. My father taught me, "all things in moderation." I think I've stuck to that where alcohol is concerned.

> The body can more easily recover from only moderate abuse. The saying is therefore useful. Nevertheless, I'll stick to my original statement: the body was not meant to intake alcohol.

But even some medicines contain alcohol!

> I have no control over what you call medicine. I'll stay with my statement.

You really are rigid, aren't You?

> Look, truth is truth. Now if someone said "A little alcohol won't hurt you," and placed that statement in the context of life as you now live it, I would have to agree with them. That does not change the truth of what I've said. It simply allows you to ignore it.
>
> Yet consider this. Currently, you humans wear your bodies out, typically, within 50 to 80 years. Some last longer, but not many. Some stop functioning sooner, but not the majority. Can we agree on that?

Yes, okay.

Alright, so we have a good starting point for discussion. Now, when I said I could agree with the statement "A little alcohol won't hurt you," I qualified that by adding "in the context of life *as you now live it*." You see, you people seem *satisfied* with life as you now live it. But life, it may surprise you to learn, was meant to be lived a whole different way. And your body was designed to last a *great deal longer*.

It was?

Yes.

How much longer?

Infinitely longer.

What does that mean?

It means, My son, your body was designed to last forever.

Forever?

Yes. Read that: "for ever more."

You mean we were—are—never supposed to die?

You never *do* die. Life is eternal. You are immortal. You never *do* die. You simply change form. You didn't even have to do that. *You* decided to do that, *I* didn't. I made you bodies that would last *forever*. Do you really think the best God could do, the best I could come up with, was a body that could make it 60, 70, maybe 80 years before falling apart? Is that, do you imagine, the limit of My ability?

I never thought of putting it that way, exactly. . .

I designed your magnificent body to last *forever!*
And the earliest of you *did* live in the body virtually
pain-free, and without fear of what you now call death.

In your religious mythology, you symbolize your
cellular memory of these first-version humans by calling
them Adam and Eve. Actually, of course, there were
more than two.

At the outset, the idea was for you wonderful souls
to have a chance to know your Selves as Who You Really
Are through experiences gained in the physical body, in
the relative world—as I have explained repeatedly here.

This was done through the slowing down of the
unfathomable speed of all vibration (thought form) to
produce matter—including that matter you call the
physical body.

Life evolved through a series of steps in the blink of
an eye that you now call billions of years. And in this
holy instant came you, out of the sea, the water of life,
onto the land and into the form you now hold.

Then the evolutionists are *right!*

I find it amusing—a source of continual amusement,
actually—that you humans have such a need to break
everything down into right and wrong. It never occurs
to you that you've *made those labels up* to help you
define the material—and your Self.

It never occurs to you (except to the finest minds
among you) that a thing could be both right *and* wrong;
that only in the relative world are things one or the
other. In the world of the absolute, of time-no time, *all
things are everything.*

There is no male and female, there is no before and
after, there is no fast and slow, here and there, up and
down, left and right—and no right and wrong.

Your astronauts and cosmonauts have gained a sense of this. They imagined themselves to be rocketing *upward* to get to outer space, only to find when they got there that they were looking *up at the Earth*. Or *were* they? Maybe they were looking *down* at the Earth! But then, where was the sun? Up? Down? No! Over there, to the *left*. So now, suddenly, a thing was neither up *nor* down—it was *sideways*. . .and all definitions thus *disappeared*.

So it is in My world— *our* world   our real realm. All definitions disappear, rendering it difficult to even talk about this realm in definitive terms.

Religion is your attempt to speak of the unspeakable. It does not do a very good job.

No, My son, the evolutionists are *not* right. I created all of this—*all* of this—in the blink of an eye; in one holy instant—just as the creationists have said. *And*. . .it came about through a process of evolution taking billions and billions of what *you* call years, just as the evolutionists claim.

They are *both* "right." As the cosmonauts discovered, *it all depends on how you look at it*.

But the real question is: one holy instant/billions of years—what's the difference? Can you simply agree that on some of the questions of life the mystery is too great for even you to solve? Why not hold the mystery as sacred? And why not allow the sacred to be sacred, and leave it alone?

I suppose we all have an insatiable need to know.

But you *already* know! I've just *told* you! Yet you don't want to know the Truth, you want to know the truth *as you understand it*. This is the greatest barrier to your enlightenment. You think you already *know* the truth! You think you already *understand* how it is. So you agree with everything you see or hear or read that falls into the paradigm of your understanding, and reject everything which does not. And this you call learning.

This you call being open to the teachings. *Alas, you can never be open to the teachings so long as you are closed to everything save your own truth.*

Thus will this very book be called blasphemy—the work of the devil—by some.

Yet those who have ears to hear, let them listen. I tell you this: *You were not meant to ever die.* Your physical form was created as a magnificent convenience; a wonderful tool; a glorious vehicle allowing you to experience the reality you have created with your mind, that you may know the Self you have created in your soul.

The soul conceives, the mind creates, the body experiences. The circle is complete. The soul then knows itself in its own experience. If it does not like what it is experiencing (feeling), or wishes a different experience for any reason, it simply conceives of a *new* experience of Self, and, quite literally, *changes its mind.*

Soon the body finds itself in a new experience. ("I am the resurrection and the Life" was a magnificent example of this. How do you think Jesus *did* it anyway? Or do you not believe it ever happened? *Believe* it. It *happened!*)

Yet this much is so: the soul will never override the body or the mind. I made you as a three-in-one being. You are three beings in one, made in the image and likeness of Me.

The three aspects of Self are in no wise unequal to each other. Each has a function, but no function is greater than another, nor does any function actually *precede* another. All are interrelated in an exactly equal way.

Conceive—create—experience. What you conceive you create, what you create you experience, what you experience you conceive.

That is why it is said, if you can cause your body to experience something (take abundance, for example), you will soon have the feeling of it in your soul, which will conceive of itself in a new way (namely, abundant), thus presenting your mind with a new thought about that. From the new thought springs more experience, and the body begins living a new reality as a permanent state of being.

Your body, your mind, and your soul (spirit) are one. In this, you are a microcosm of Me—the Divine All, the Holy Everything, the Sum and Substance. You see now how I am the beginning and the end of everything, the Alpha and the Omega.

Now I will explain to you the ultimate mystery: your exact and true relationship to Me.

YOU ARE MY BODY.

As *your* body is to *your* mind and soul, so, too, are *you* to *My* mind and soul. Therefore:

Everything I experience, I experience through you.

Just as your body, mind, and spirit are one, so, too, are Mine.

So it is that Jesus of Nazareth, among the many who understood this mystery, spoke immutable truth when he said, *"I and the Father are One."*

Now I will tell you, there are even larger truths than this to which you will one day become privy. For even as you are the body of Me, I am the body of another.

You mean, You are *not* God?

Yes, I am God, as you now understand Him. I am Goddess as you now comprehend Her. I am the Conceiver and the Creator of Everything you now know and experience, and you are My children. . .even as I am the child of another.

Are You trying to tell me that even God has a God?

I am telling you that your perception of ultimate reality is more limited than you thought, and that Truth is more *un*limited than you can imagine.

197

I am giving you ever-so-small a glimpse of infinity—
and infinite love. (A much larger glimpse and you could
not hold it in your reality. You can barely hold *this*.)

Wait a minute! You mean I'm really *not* talking with God
here?

I have told you—if you conceive of God as your
creator and master—even as you are the creator and
master of your own body—I am the God of your
understanding. And you are talking with Me, yes. It has
been a delicious conversation, no?

Delicious or not, I thought I was talking with the real God.
The God of Gods. You know—the top guy, the chief honcho.

You are. Believe Me. You are.

And yet You say that there is someone above You in this
hierarchal scheme of things.

We are now trying to do the impossible, which is to
speak of the unspeakable. As I said, that is what religion
seeks to do. Let Me see if I can find a way to summarize
this.

Forever is longer than you know. Eternal is longer
than Forever. God is more than you imagine. God *is* the
energy you call imagination. God *is* creation. God *is* first
thought. And God *is* last experience. And God is everything in between.

Have you ever looked down a high-powered micro-
scope, or seen pictures or movies of molecular action,
and said, "Good heavens, there's a *whole universe*
down there. And to that universe, I, the now-present
observer, must feel like God!" Have you ever said that,
or had that kind of experience?

Yes, I should imagine every thinking person has.

Indeed. You have given yourself your own glimpse of what I am showing you here.

And what would you do if I told you that this reality of which you have given yourself a glimpse *never ends?*

Explain that. I'd ask You to explain that.

Take the smallest part of the universe you can imagine. Imagine this tiny, tiny particle of matter.

Okay.

Now cut it in half.

Okay.

What have you got?

Two smaller halves.

Precisely. Now cut those in half. What now?

Two *smaller* halves.

Right. Now again, and *again!* What's left?

Smaller and smaller particles.

Yes, but when does it *stop?* How many times can you divide matter until it ceases to exist?

I don't know. I guess it never ceases to exist.

You mean you can never *completely destroy* it? All you can do is change its form?

It would seem so.

I tell you this: you have just learned the secret of all of life, and seen into infinity.

Now I have a question to ask you.

Okay. . .

What makes you think infinity goes only one way?—

So. . .there is no end going up, any more than there is going down.

There *is* no up or down, but I understand your meaning.

But if there is no end to smallness, that means there is no end to bigness.

Correct.

But if there is no end to bigness, then there is no *biggest.* That means, in the largest sense, there *is no God!*

Or, perhaps—*all of it is God,* and *there is nothing else.*

I tell you this: I AM THAT I AM.

And YOU ARE THAT YOU ARE. You cannot *not be.* You can change form all you wish, but you cannot fail to be. Yet you *can* fail to *know* Who You Are—and in this failing, experience *only the half of it.*

That would be hell.

Exactly. Yet you are not condemned to it. You are not relegated to it forevermore. All that it takes to get out of hell—to get out of not knowing—is to know again.

There are many ways and many places (dimensions) in which you can do this.

You are in one of those dimensions now. It is called, in your understanding, the third dimension.

And there are many more?

Have I not told you that in My Kingdom there are many mansions? I would not have told it to you were it not so.

Then there *is* no hell—not really. I mean, there *is* no place or dimension to which we are everlastingly condemned!

What would be the purpose of that?

Yet you are always limited by your knowingness—for you—we—are a self-created being.

You cannot be what you do not know your Self to be.

That is why you have been given this life—so that you might know yourself in your own experience. Then you can conceive of yourself as Who You Really Are, and create yourself as that in your experience—and the circle is again complete. . .only bigger.

And so, you are in the process of growing—or, as I have put it throughout this book, of *becoming*.

There is *no limit* to what you can become.

You mean, I can even become—dare I say it?—a God. . .just like You?

What do *you* think?

I don't know.

Until you do, you cannot. Remember the triangle—the Holy Trinity: spirit-mind-body. Conceive-create-experience. Remember, using your symbology:

HOLY SPIRIT = INSPIRATION = CONCEIVE
FATHER = PARENTING = CREATE
SON = OFFSPRING = EXPERIENCE

The Son experiences the creation of the fathering thought, which is conceived of by the Holy Ghost.

Can you conceive of yourself as one day being a God?

In my wildest moments.

Good, for I tell you this: You are *already* a God. *You simply do not know it.*

Have I not said, "Ye are Gods"?

14

There now. I have explained it all for you. Life. How it works. Its very reason and purpose. How else can I serve you?

There's nothing more I could ask. I am filled with thanks for this incredible dialogue. It's been so far-reaching, so encompassing. And, as I look at my original questions, I see we've covered the first five—having to do with life and relationships, money and careers, and health. I had more questions on that original list, as you know, but somehow these discussions make those questions seem irrelevant.

Yes. Still, you've asked them. Let's just quickly answer the remainder of them, one by one. Now that we're moving this rapidly through the material—

—What material?—

The material I brought you here to expose you to—now that we're moving this rapidly though the material, let's just take those remaining questions and deal with them quickly.

6. What is the karmic lesson I'm supposed to be learning here? What am I trying to master?

You are learning nothing here. You have nothing to learn. You have only to remember. That is, re-member Me.
What are you trying to master? You are trying to master *mastering itself*.

7. Is there such a thing as reincarnation? How many past lives have I had? What was I in them? Is "karmic debt" a reality?

It is difficult to believe there is still a question about this. I find it hard to imagine. There have been so many reports from thoroughly reliable sources of past life experiences. Some of these people have brought back strikingly detailed descriptions of events, and such completely verifiable data as to eliminate any possibility that they were making it up or had contrived to somehow deceive researchers and loved ones.

You have had 647 past lives, since you insist on being exact. This is your 648th. You were *everything* in them. A king, a queen, a serf. A teacher, a student, a master. A male, a female. A warrior, a pacifist. A hero, a coward. A killer, a savior. A sage, a fool. You have been *all* of it!

No, there is no such thing as karmic debt—not in the sense that you mean in this question. A debt is something that must or should be repaid. *You are not obligated to do anything.*

Still, there are certain things that you *want* to do; *choose* to experience. And some of these choices hinge on—the desire for them has been created by—what you have experienced before.

That is as close as words can come to this thing you call karma.

If karma is the innate desire to be better, to be bigger, to evolve and to grow, and to look at past events and experiences as a measure of that, then, yes, karma does exist.

But it does not require anything. Nothing is ever required. You are, as always you have ever been, a being of free choice.

8. I sometimes feel very psychic. Is there such a thing as being psychic? Am I that? Are people who claim to be psychic "trafficking with the devil"?

Yes, there is such a thing as being psychic. You *are* that. *Everyone* is that. There is not a person who does not have what you call psychic ability, there are only people who do not use it.

Using psychic ability is nothing more than using your sixth sense.

Obviously, this is not "trafficking with the devil," or I would not have *given* this sense to you. And, of course, there *is* no devil with whom to traffic.

Someday—perhaps in Book Two—I'll explain to you exactly how psychic energy and psychic ability works.

There is going to be a Book Two?

Yes. But let's finish this one first.

9. Is it okay to take money for doing good? If I choose to do healing work in the world—God's work—can I do that and become financially abundant, too? Or are the two mutually exclusive?

I've already covered this.

10. Is sex okay? C'mon—what is the real story behind this human experience? Is sex purely for procreation, as some religions say? Is true holiness and enlightenment achieved through denial—or transmutation—of the sexual energy? Is it okay to have sex without love? Is just the physical sensation of it okay enough as a reason?

Of course sex is "okay." Again, if I didn't want you to play certain games, I wouldn't have given you the toys. Do you give your children things you don't want them to play with?

Play with sex. *Play* with it! It's *wonderful* fun. Why, it's just about the most fun you can *have* with your body, if you're talking of strictly physical experiences alone.

But for goodness sake, don't destroy sexual innocence and pleasure and the purity of the fun, the joy, by misusing sex. Don't use it for power, or hidden purpose; for ego gratification or domination; for any purpose other than the purest joy and the highest ecstasy, given and shared—which is *love,* and love *recreated*—which is new life! Have I not chosen a delicious way to *make more of you?*

With regard to denial, I have dealt with that before. Nothing holy has ever been achieved through denial. Yet *desires* change as even larger realities are glimpsed. It is not unusual, therefore, for people to simply *desire* less, or even no, sexual activity—or, for that matter, *any* of a number of activities of the body. For some, the activities of the soul become foremost—and by far the more pleasurable.

Each to his own, without judgment—that is the motto.

The end of your question is answered this way: You don't need to have a reason for anything. Just *be cause.*

Be the cause of your experience.

Remember, experience produces concept of Self, conception produces creation, creation produces experience.

You want to experience yourself as a person who has sex without love? Go ahead! You'll do that until you don't want to anymore. And the only thing that will—that could *ever*—cause you to stop this, or *any,* behavior, is your newly emerging thought about Who You Are.

It's as simple—and as complex—as that.

11. Why did You make sex so good, so spectacular, so powerful a human experience if all we are to do is stay away from it as much as we can? What gives? For that matter, why are all fun things either "immoral, illegal, or fattening"?

I've answered the end of this question too, with what I've just said. All fun things are *not* immoral, illegal, or fattening. Your life is, however, an interesting exercise in defining what fun is.

To some, "fun" means sensations of the body. To others, "fun" may be something entirely different. It all depends on who you think you are, and what you are doing here.

There is much more to be said about sex than is being said here—but nothing more essential than this: sex is *joy*, and many of you have made sex everything else but.

Sex is sacred, too—yes. But joy and sacredness *do* mix (they are, in fact, the same thing), and many of you think they do not.

Your attitudes about sex form a microcosm of your attitudes about life. Life should be a joy, a celebration, and it has become an experience of fear, anxiety, "not enough-ness," envy, rage, and tragedy. The same can be said about sex.

You have repressed sex, even as you have repressed life, rather than fully Self expressing, with abandon and joy.

You have shamed sex, even as you have shamed life, calling it evil and wicked, rather than the highest gift and the greatest pleasure.

Before you protest that you have not shamed life, look at your collective attitudes about it. Four-fifths of the world's people consider life a trial, a tribulation, a time of testing, a karmic debt that must be paid, a school with harsh lessons that must be learned, and, in general, an experience to be endured while awaiting the *real* joy, which is *after death*.

It *is* a shame that so many of you *think* this way. Small wonder you have applied shame to the very act which creates life.

The energy which underscores sex is the energy which underscores life; which *is* life! The feeling of attraction and the intense and often urgent desire to move *toward* each other, to become one, is the essential dynamic of all that lives. I have built it into every-

207

thing. It is inbred, inherent, _inside_ All That Is.

The moral codes, religious constrictions, social taboos, and emotional conventions you have placed around sex (and, by the way, around love—and all of life) have made it virtually impossible for you to _celebrate your being._

From the beginning of time all man has ever wanted is to love and be loved. And from the beginning of time man has done everything in his power to make it impossible to do that. Sex is an extraordinary expression of love—love of another, love of Self, love of _life_. You ought to therefore _love_ it! (And you _do_—you just can't _tell_ anyone you do; you don't dare _show_ how _much_ you love it, or you'll be called a pervert. Yet _this_ is the idea that is _perverted._)

In our next book, we shall look at sex much more closely; explore its dynamics in greater detail, for this is an experience and an issue of sweeping implications on a global scale.

For now—and for you, personally—simply know this: _I have given you nothing shameful, least of all your very body, and its functions. There is no need to hide your body or its functions—nor your love of them, and of each other._

Your television programs think nothing of showing naked violence, but shrink from showing naked love. Your whole society reflects that priority.

12. Is there life on other planets? Have we been visited by it? Are we being observed now? Will we see evidence—irrevocable and indisputable—of extraterrestrial life in our lifetime? Does each form of life have its own God? Are You the God of it all?

Yes to the first part. Yes to the second. Yes to the third. I cannot answer the fourth part, since that would require Me to predict the future—something I am not going to do.

We will, however, talk a great deal more about this thing called the future in Book Two—and we'll talk about extraterrestrial life and the nature(s) of God in Book Three.

Ohmigosh. There's going to be a Book _Three?_

Let me outline the plan here.

Book One is to contain basic truths, primary understandings, and address essential personal matters and issues.

Book Two is to contain more far-reaching truths, grander understandings, and address global matters and issues.

Book Three is to contain the largest truths you are now capable of understanding, and address universal matters and issues—matters being dealt with by all the beings of the universe.

I see. This is an order?

No. If you can ask that question you have understood nothing in this book.

You have _chosen_ to do this work—and you have _been_ chosen. The circle is complete.

Do you understand?

Yes.

13. Will utopia ever come to the planet Earth? Will God ever show Himself to Earth's people, as promised? Is there such a thing as the Second Coming? Will there ever be an end of the world—or an apocalypse, as prophesied in the Bible? Is there a one true religion? If so, which one?

That's a book in itself, and will comprise much of Volume Three. I've kept this opening volume limited to more personal matters, more practical issues. I'll move to larger questions and matters of global and universal implication in succeeding installments.

Is that it? Is that all for now? Are we to speak no more here?

You miss me already?

I do! This has been fun! Are we quitting now?

You need a little rest. And your readers need a rest, too. There's a lot here to absorb. A lot to wrestle with. A lot to ponder. Take some time off. Reflect on this. Ponder it.

Do not feel abandoned. I am always with you. If you have questions—day-to-day questions—as I know you do even now, and will continue to—know that you can call on Me to answer them. You do not need the form of this book.

This is not the only way I speak to you. Listen to Me in the truth of your soul. Listen to Me in the feelings of your heart. Listen to Me in the quiet of your mind.

Hear Me, everywhere. Whenever you have a question, simply know that I have answered it already. Then open your eyes to your world. My response could be in an article already published. In the sermon already written and about to be delivered. In the movie now being made. In the song just yesterday composed. In the words about to be said by a loved one. In the heart of a new friend about to be made.

My Truth is in the whisper of the wind, the babble of the brook, the crack of the thunder, the tap of the rain.

It is the feel of the earth, the fragrance of the lily, the warmth of the sun, the pull of the moon.

My Truth—and your surest help in time of need—is as awesome as the night sky, and as simply, incontrovertibly, trustful as a baby's gurgle.

It is as loud as a pounding heartbeat—and as quiet as a breath taken in unity with Me.

I will not leave you, I *cannot* leave you, for you are
My creation and My product, My daughter and My son,
My purpose and My. . .
Self.

Call on Me, therefore, wherever and whenever you
are separate from the peace that I am.

I will be there.

With Truth.

And Light.

And Love.

In Closing

Since receiving the information contained in this book, and quietly spreading the word about it, I have answered many inquiries, both about how it was received and about the dialogue itself. I honor every inquiry, and the sincerity with which it is made. People simply want to know more about this, and that is understandable.

While I wish I could take every phone call and personally respond to every letter, it is just not possible to do that. Among other things, I would be spending a great deal of time answering essentially the same questions over and over again. So I've thought about how I could interact with you more efficiently, and still honor each inquiry.

What I've decided is to write a monthly letter to those with questions or comments regarding this dialogue. In this way it is possible for me to respond to all the inquiries which come in and to react to all the commentaries, without having to write many, many individual letters each month. I know this may not be the best way to communicate with you, and it certainly is not the most personal, but it is what I am now capable of doing.

The monthly letter is available upon request to:

ReCreation
Postal Drawer 3475
Central Point, Oregon 97502

In the beginning this letter was made available at no fee, but we never dreamed so many would ask for it. Because of the mounting costs, we are now asking for a minimal donation of twenty-five dollars per year so that we can continue to reach as many people as possible. If you are unable financially to help us with these costs, please ask for a scholarship subscription.

I'm glad you have been able to share this extraordinary dialogue with me. I wish you the highest experience of life's rich blessings, and an awareness of God in your life that brings you peace, joy, and love through all your days and endeavors.

Neale Donald Walsch

Index

relationships *(continued)*
    getting lost in, 125
    to God, 197
    greatest gift from God, 24
    longevity, 138, 140
    and obligation, 135, 137, 138
    only relevant question, 130
    pain, dealing with, 128, 133-134
    paradox of, 123
    purpose of, 122, 126
    putting Self first, 124-125, 132
    romantic, 122-125
    as sacred, 124, 126, 138
    and suffering, 134
    why they fail, 122, 142
relativity, 15, 24, 27, 56, 134
religion
    and creation, 26
    attractions of, 155
    and fear, 154-155
    fundamentalist, 136, 137
    interest in status quo, 48
    and killing, 153
    misconception of, 119
    and opportunity/obligation, 137
    provides approval, 155
    role of, 49, 195
    and sin, 85
    "weird, vindictive, angry," 120
    what they tell you, 154
    why popular, 152
renunciation, 100, 104
    See also self-denial
resistance, 100, 103
results, attachment to, 101-102, 110
retribution, 41-42
Revelation, 9-10, 58
"right" and "wrong," 7, 39, 40, 47, 62, 84, 109, 122, 152, 154, 162
rules of life, 41

S

sacred law of universe, 47
salvation, 18, 51, 119, 127, 136, 175
samadhi, 102
Satan. *See* devil
school. *See* life, as school
scriptures, holy. *See* holy scriptures

secret of life, 20
Self centeredness, 124, 132
self-denial, 82-83, 100
self-hate. *See* hate, of self
self-love, 132
Self realization, 52, 76, 102, 113, 116, 129, 180
self-worth, 126, 160
sex, judgments about, 86, 108-109, 205-208
sexual taboos, 51
sexuality, 63
Shakespeare, 43
shame, 119
    and life, 207
    and sex, 207
"should" and "shouldn't," 38-39, 169
sin, 38, 62, 85, 119, 136
smoking, 187, 191
soul
    challenge of, 77
    choosing destiny, 114
    defined, 74
    desire of, 22, 170, 172-174, 180
    freedom to walk own path, 47
    knowledge of, 22
    language of, 3
    listening to, 81
    purpose of, 28, 43, 82-83, 102, 116, 126, 196
    relationship to body and mind, 174, 175
    relationship to calamity, 32
    as Who You Are, 130
space, 73
spirits, 25
"spiritual game," 113
spiritual path, 100
    why follow, 156
spirituality, basis of, 137
Sponsoring Thought, 12, 16, 18, 167
    changing, 164, 167
starvation. *See* famine
stress, 187
strokes, 187
struggle, 115
    fostering religion, 51
subconscious, 31
success, 176, 180
suffering, 47, 107, 131

About the Artists

Louis Jones is a native of Tidewater, Virginia. His egg temperas, watercolors, and drawings reflect his love of nature and his love for people—capturing, as he describes, "the moving skies, the fluid landscapes . . .the discarded homes and faded dreams of rural America." Jones's work has been shown in galleries throughout the United States and Europe, and he was one of the select few American artists to display at the Contemporary Art Exhibit in Bath, England. He has been included in *American Artists of Renown.*

Elizabeth Hinshaw is a self-taught portrait artist who specializes in charcoal and pastel pencils. For fifteen years she has been showing her art and accepting commissions from corporate and private clients around the world. Elizabeth may be reached at P.O. Box 585, Ashland, OR 97520, (541) 488-2137.

For a limited edition reprint of the original cover painting, The Lake, *by Louis Jones, please write to:*

The Louis & Susan Jones Art Gallery
Dominion Tower
999 Waterside Dr
Norfolk, VA 23510.

Or call (804) 625-6505 for further information.